AF308460

FSC
www.fsc.org
MIXTE
Papier issu
de sources
responsables
Paper from
responsible sources
FSC® C105338

Building a minimal reflective kernel

Stéphane Ducasse

November 9, 2024

Keepers of the light house
Édition : BoD · Books on Demand GmbH, In de Tarpen 42, 22848 Norderstedt (Allemagne)
Impression : Libri Plureos GmbH, Friedensallee 273, 22763 Hamburg (Allemagne)
ISBN : 978-2-3225-0618-7
Dépôt légal : Novembre 2024
Layout and typography based on the sbabook LaTeX class by Damien Pollet.

Contents

Back in the early 90's, when I was a student, built a theorem proving system in Common Lisp Object System. It was a fun first contact with object-oriented programming, even if at the time I did not master all the aspects. The following year, we got an excellent lecture on meta-object programming by M. Blay Fornarino. I loved the lecture where we program metaclasses and mixins. I realize now that it was quite advanced.

However, deep inside me, I knew that I did not fully understand what was the class Object or what was really a metaclass. Of course, I could repeat the lecture and look smart, but there was this little voice telling me that I wasn't 100% sure. Then, I read the article of Pierre Cointe on ObjVlisp. I got blasted by the simplicity of the model. I spent the next 2 days reimplementing the model because it was too much fun. For me, it is the key to my deep understanding of class-based reflective systems. Once I finished implementing it, I went to see my teacher and told her that she must teach it. She told me to do it. Since then I've been teaching it.

Note that while the project is historically named ObjVlisp, it has not much to do with LISP. This kernel is similar to the one of Smalltalk-78 with explicit metaclasses. ObjVlisp is just a little conceptual framework but it provides a condensed view and explains the forces present in larger systems such as Pharo that share the *everything is an object* mantra I love so much.

This book explains the consequence of having classes as objects. In addition, it describes the design and the consequences of having a self-described reflective minimal kernel.

By doing so we will learn deeply about objects, object creation instantiation, message lookup, delegation, inheritance, and much more.

I would like to thank Christopher Fuhrman for his large copy-edit pass and kksubbu, Imen Sayar, and René-Paul for their suggestions.

— Stéphane Ducasse

CHAPTER 1

A minimal reflective class-based kernel

The difference between classes and objects has been repeatedly emphasized. In the view presented here, these concepts belong to different worlds: the program text only contains classes; at run-time, only objects exist. This is not the only approach. One of the subcultures of object-oriented programming, influenced by Lisp and exemplified by Smalltalk, views classes as objects themselves, which still have an existence at run-time.
— B. Meyer, Object-Oriented Software Construction [6]

As this quote expresses it, there is a realm where classes are true objects, instances of other classes. In such systems as Smalltalk, Pharo [1], CLOS [7], classes are described by other classes and form often reflective architectures each one describing the previous level. In this chapter, we will explore a minimal reflective class-based kernel, inspired by ObjVlisp. In the following chapter, you will implement step by step such a kernel with less than 30 methods.

1.1 ObjVlisp inspiration

ObjVlisp was published for the first time in 1987 when the foundation of object-oriented programming was still emerging [3]. ObjVlisp has explicit metaclasses and supports metaclass reuse. It was inspired by the kernel of Smalltalk-78. The IBM SOM-DSOM kernel is similar to ObjVLisp while implemented in C++ [4]. ObjVlisp is a subset of the reflective kernel of CLOS (Common Lisp Object System) since CLOS reifies instance variables, generic functions, and method combinations. It is the equivalent of the Closette implementation [5]. In comparison to ObjVlisp, Smalltalk, and Pharo have implicit metaclasses and no metaclass reuse except by basic inheritance. However, they are more stable as explained by Bouraqadi et al [2].

Studying this kernel is really worth it since it has the following properties:

- It unifies classes and instances (there is only one data structure to represent all objects, classes included).

- It is composed of only two classes `Class` and `Object` (it relies on existing elements such as booleans, arrays, and strings of the underlying implementation language).

- It raises the question of meta-circularity infinite regression (a class is an instance of another class that is an instance of yet another class, etc.) and how to resolve it.

- It requires consideration of allocation, class, and object initialization, message passing as well as the bootstrap process.

- It can be implemented in less than 30 methods in Pharo.

Just remember that this kernel is self-described. We will start to explain some aspects, but since everything is linked, you may have to read the chapter twice to fully get it.

1.2 ObjVLisp's six postulates

The original ObjVlisp kernel is defined by six postulates [3]. Some of them look a bit dated by modern standards, and the 6th postulate is simply wrong as we will explain later (a solution is simple to design and implement).

Here are the six postulates as stated in the paper for the sake of historical perspective.

- P1. An object represents a piece of knowledge and a set of capabilities.

-P2 . The only protocol to activate an object is message passing: a message specifies which procedure to apply (denoted by its name, the selector) and its arguments.

- P3. Every object belongs to a class that specifies its data (attributes called fields) and its behavior (procedures called methods). Objects will be dynamically generated from this model; they are called instances of the class. Following Plato, all instances of a class have the same structure and shape but differ through the values of their common instance variables.

- P4. A class is also an object, instantiated by another class, called its metaclass. Consequently (P3), to each class is associated with a metaclass which describes its behavior as an object. The initial primitive metaclass is the class `Class`, built as its own instance.

- P5. A class can be defined as a subclass of one (or many) other class(es). This subclassing mechanism allows the sharing of instance variables and methods and is called inheritance. The class `Object` represents the most common behavior shared by all objects.

- P6. If the instance variables owned by an object define a local environment, there are also class variables defining a global environment shared by all the instances of the same class. These class variables are defined at the metaclass level according to the following equation: class variable [an-object] = instance variable [an-object's class].

1.3   Kernel overview

If you do not fully grasp the following overview, don't worry. This full chapter is here to make sure that you will understand it. Let us get started.

Contrary to a real uniform language kernel, ObjVlisp does not consider arrays, booleans, strings, numbers or any other elementary objects as part of the kernel as this is the case in a real bootstrap such as the one of Pharo. ObjVLisp's kernel focuses on understanding `Class`/`Object` core relationships.

Figure 1-1 shows the two core classes of the kernel:

- `Object` which is the root of the inheritance graph and is an instance of `Class`.

- `Class` is the first class and root of the instantiation tree and instance of itself as we will see later.

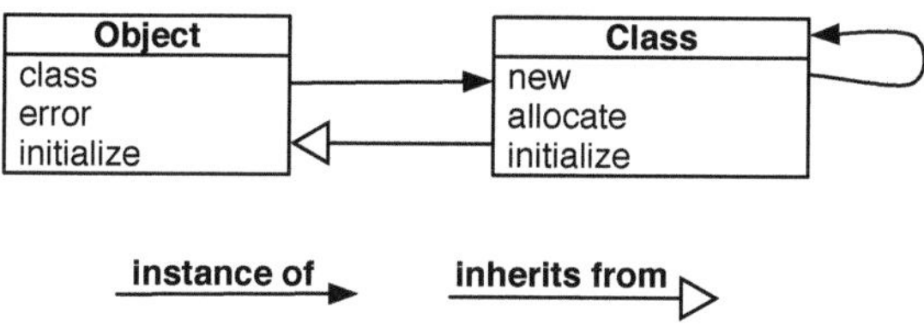

Figure 1-1   The ObjVlisp kernel: a minimal class-based kernel.

Figure 1-2 shows that the class `Workstation` is an instance of the class `Class` since it is a class and it inherits from `Object` the default behavior objects should exhibit. The class `WithSingleton` is an instance of the class `Class` but in addition, it inherits from `Class`, since this is a metaclass: its instances are classes. As such, it changes the behavior of classes. The class `SpecialWorkstation` is an instance of the class `WithSingleton` and inherits from `Workstation`, since its instances exhibit the same behavior as `Workstation`.

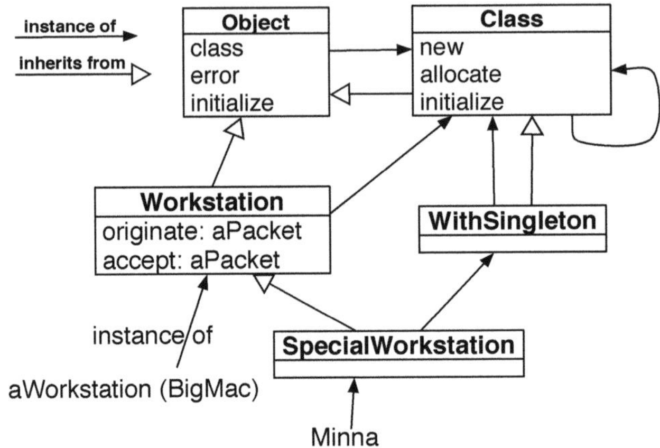

Figure 1-2   The kernel with specialized metaclasses.

The two diagrams 1-1 and 1-2 will be explained step by step throughout this chapter.

> **Note**   The key point of understanding such a reflective architecture is that message passing always looks up methods in the class of the receiver of the message and then follows the inheritance chain (See Figure 1-3).

Figure 1-3 illustrates two main cases:

- When we send a message to `BigMac` or `Minna`, the corresponding method is looked up in their corresponding classes `Workstation` or `Special-Workstation` and follows the inheritance link up to `Object`.

- When we send a message to the classes `Workstation` or `SpecialWork-station`, the corresponding method is looked up in their class, the class `Class` and up to `Object`.

1.4   Conclusion

ObjVLisp is a minimal kernel with its two main classes. It uses the infrastructure of the underlying language (integers, strings, booleans...). When the language is fully reflective such as Pharo all such infrastructure has to be defined at the same level as the class `Object` and `Class` but the model principles stay the same.

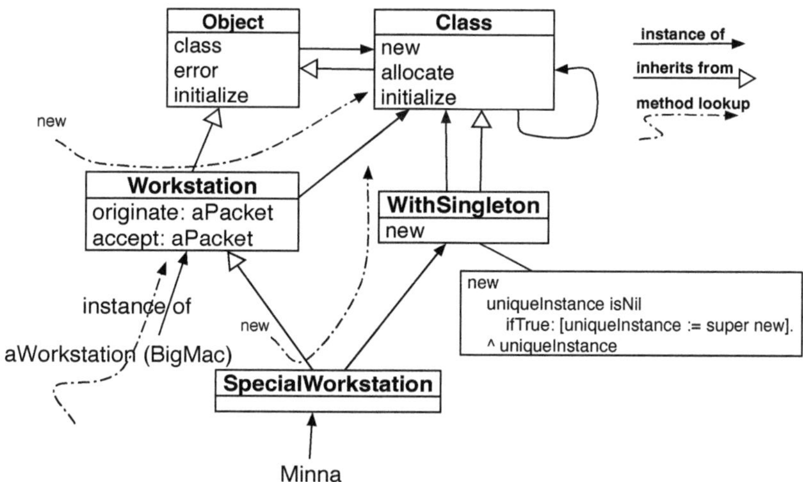

Figure 1-3   Understanding metaclasses using message passing.

CHAPTER 2

Diving into the kernel

In this chapter, we will describe one by one all the aspects of the kernel. We will cover instance shapes, methods, instance and inheritance relationship interplay, object allocation, object and class initialization...

2.1 Instances

In this kernel, there is only one instantiation link; it is applied at all levels as shown by Figure 2-1:

- Terminal instances are objects: a workstation named mac1 is an instance of the class Workstation, a point 10@20 is an instance of the class Point.

- Classes are also objects (instances) of other classes: the class Workstation is an instance of the class Class, and the class Point is an instance of the class Class.

In our diagrams, we represent objects (mainly terminal instances) as rounded rectangles with a list of instance variable values. Since classes are objects, *when we want to stress that classes are objects* we use the same graphical convention as shown in Figure 2-4.

Handling infinite recursion

A class is an object. Thus it is an instance of another class, its metaclass. This metaclass is an object, too, an instance of a metametaclass that is an object, too, an instance of another metametametaclass, etc. To stop this potential infi-

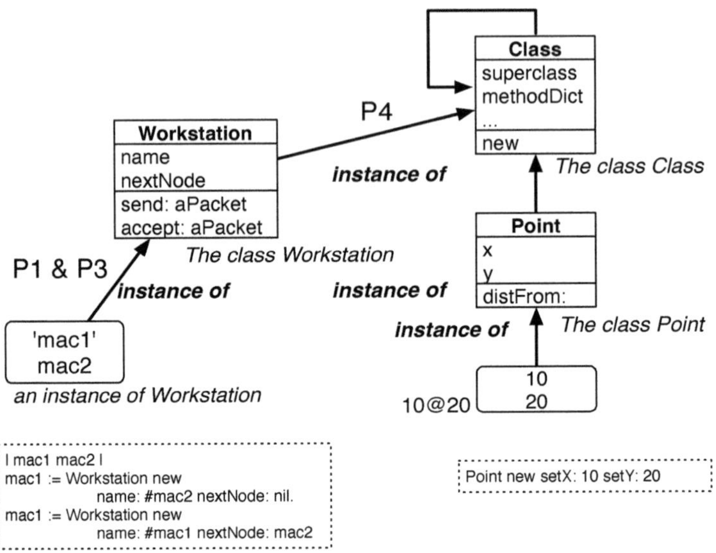

Figure 2-1   Chain of instantiation: classes are objects, too.

nite recursion, ObjVlisp is similar to solutions proposed in many meta-circular systems: one instance (e.g., Class) is an instance of itself.

In ObjVLisp:

- Class is the initial class and metaclass,

- Class is an instance of itself, and, directly or indirectly, all other meta-classes are instances of Class.

We will see later the implication of this self-instantiation at the level of the class structure itself.

2.2   Understanding metaclasses

The model unifies classes and instances. It follows from the instance-related postulates of the kernel that:

- Every object is an instance of a class,

- A class is an object instance of a metaclass, and

- A metaclass is only a class that generates classes.

At the implementation level, there is only one kind of entity: objects. There is no special treatment for classes. Classes are instantiated following the same process as terminal instances. They are sent messages in the same way that other objects are sent messages.

This unification between instances and classes does not mean that objects and classes have the same distinction. Indeed not all the objects are classes. In particular, the sole difference between a class and an instance is the ability to respond to the creation message: new. Only a class knows how to respond to it. Then, metaclasses are just classes whose instances are classes as shown in Figure 2-2.

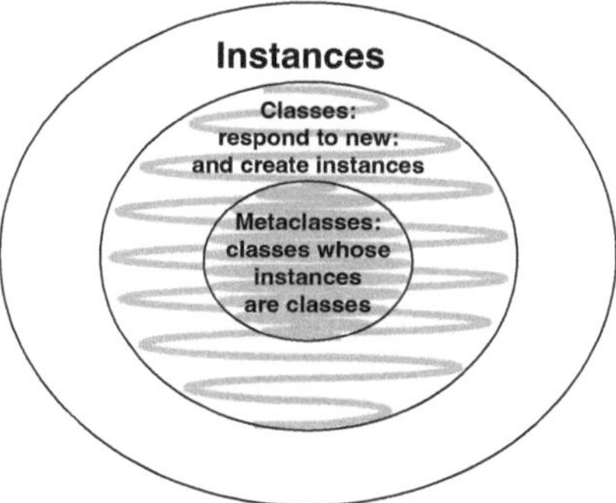

Figure 2-2 Everything is an object. Classes are just objects that can create other objects, and metaclasses are just classes whose instances are classes.

2.3 Instance structure

The model does not really bring anything new about instance structure when compared with languages such as Pharo or Java.

Instance variables are represented as a list of instance variable defined by a class. Such instance variables are shared by all instances. The *values* of such instance variables are specific to each instance. Figure 2-3 shows that instances of Workstation have two values: a name and a next node.

In addition, we note that an object has a pointer to its class. As we will see when we discuss inheritance later on, every object possesses an instance variable class (inherited from Object) that points to its class.

Note that this management of a class instance variable defined in Object is specific to the model. In Pharo for example, the class identification is not managed as a declared instance variable, but as an element part of any object. It is an index in a class table.

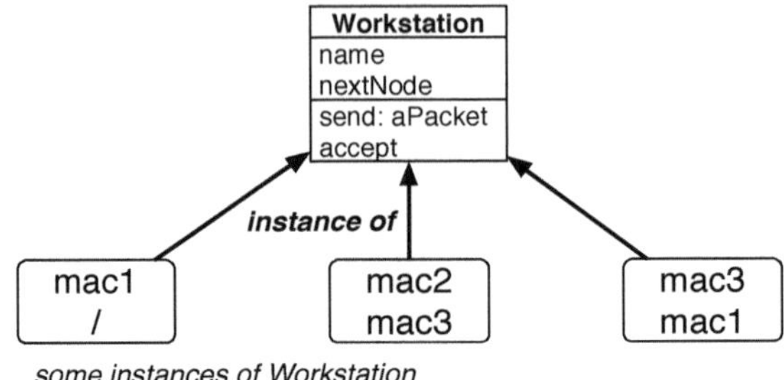

Figure 2-3 Instances of Workstation have two values: their names and their next node.

2.4 About behavior

Let us continue with basic instance behavior. As in modern class-based languages, this kernel has to represent how methods are stored and looked up.

Methods belong to a class. They define the behavior of all the instances of the class. They are stored in a method dictionary that associates a key (the method selector) and the method body.

Since methods are stored in a class, the method dictionary should be described in the metaclass. Therefore, the method dictionary of a class is the *value* of the instance variable methodDict defined on the metaclass Class. Each class will have its own method dictionary.

2.5 Class as an object

Here is the minimal information that a class should have:

- A list of instance variables to describe the values that the instances will hold,

- A method dictionary to hold methods,

- A superclass to look up inherited methods.

This minimal state is similar to that of Pharo: the Pharo Behavior class has a format (compact description of instance variables), a method dictionary, and a superclass link.

In ObjVLisp, we have a name to identify the class. As an instance factory, the metaclass Class possesses four instance variables that describe a class:

- name, the class name,

- superclass, its superclass (we limit to single inheritance),

- iv, the list of its instance variables, and

- methodDict, a method dictionary.

Since a class is an object, a class has the instance variable class inherited from Object that refers to its class as any object.

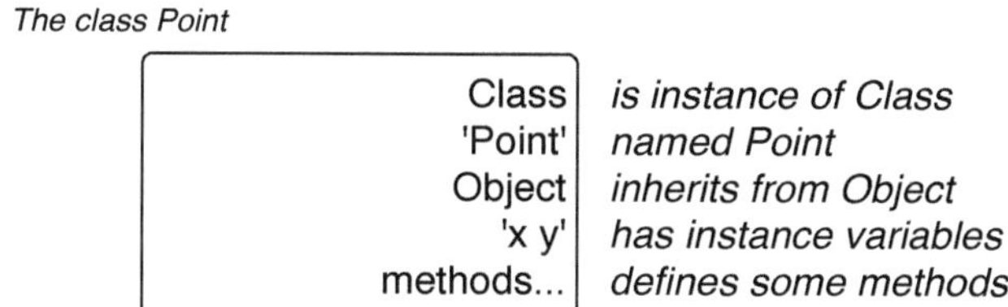

Figure 2-4   Point class as an object.

Example 1: class Point

Figure 2-4 shows the instance variable values for the class Point as declared by the programmer and before class initialization and inheritance take place.

- It is an instance of class Class: indeed this is a class.

- It is named 'Point'.

- It inherits from class Object.

- It has two instance variables: x and y. Once the static inheritance of instance variables occurs, it will be three instance variables: class, x, and y.

- It has a method dictionary.

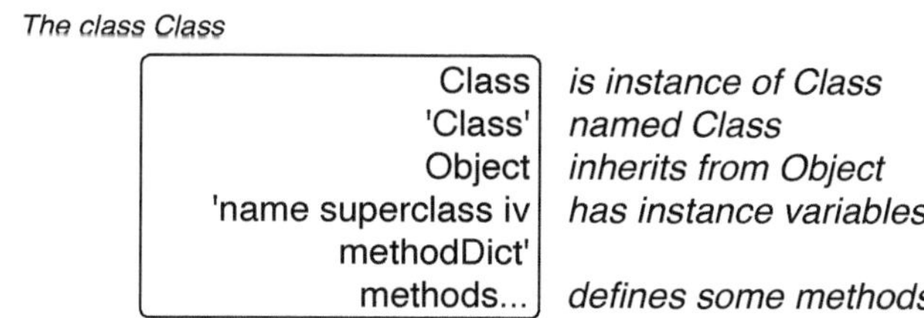

Figure 2-5   Class as an object.

Example 2: class Class

Figure 2-5 describes the class Class itself. Indeed it is also an object.

- It is an instance of class Class: indeed this is a class.

- It is named 'Class'.

- It inherits from class Object

- It has four locally defined instance variables: name, superclass, iv, and methodDict.

- It has a method dictionary.

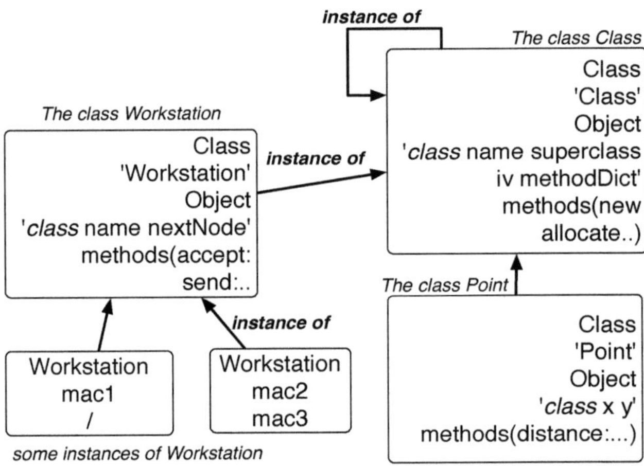

Figure 2-6   Through the prism of objects.

Everything is an object

Figure 2-6 describes a typical situation of terminal instances, classes, and meta-classes when viewed from an object perspective. We see three levels of instances: terminal objects (mac1 and mac2 which are instances of Workstation), class objects (Workstation and Point which are instances of Class) and the metaclass (Class which is an instance of itself).

2.6   Sending a message

In this kernel, the second postulate states that the only way to perform computation is via message passing.

Sending a message is a two-step process as shown by Figure 2-7:

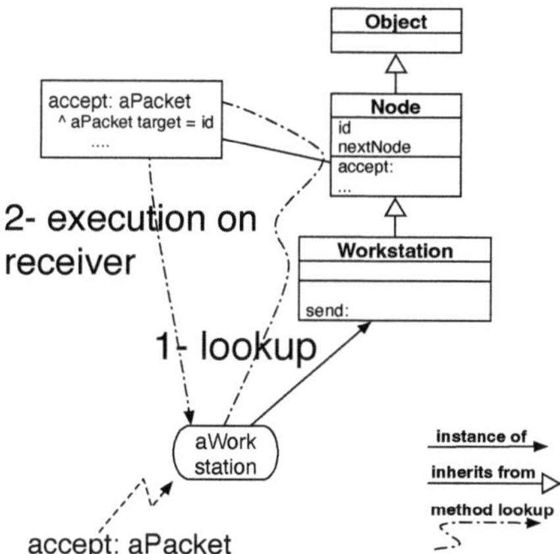

Figure 2-7   Sending a message is a two-step process: method lookup and execution.

1. Method lookup: the method corresponding to the selector is looked up in the class of the receiver and its superclasses.

2. Method execution: the method is applied to the receiver. This means that `self` or `this` in the method will be bound to the receiver.

Conceptually, sending a message can be described by the following function composition:

```
sending a message (receiver argument)
   return apply (lookup (selector classof(receiver) receiver) receiver
      arguments)
```

Method lookup

Now the lookup process is conceptually defined as follows:

1. The lookup starts in the **class** of the **receiver.**

2. If the method is defined in that class (i.e., if the method is defined in the method dictionary), it is returned.

3. Otherwise the search continues in the superclass of the currently explored class.

4. If no method is found and there is no superclass to explore (if we are in the class `Object`), this is an error (i.e., the method is not defined).

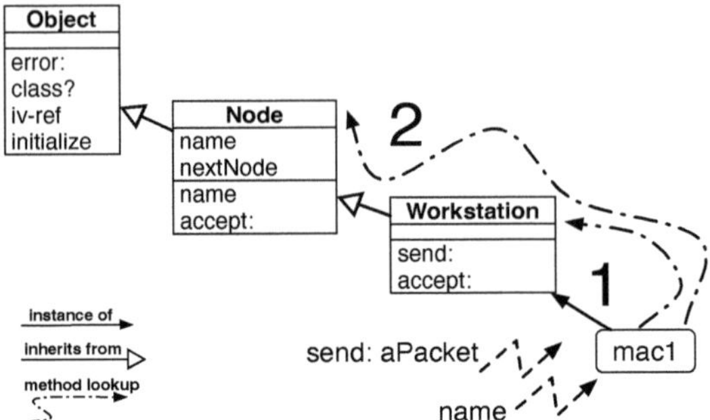

Figure 2-8 Looking for a method is a two-step process: first, go to the class of receiver then follow inheritance.

The method lookup walks through the inheritance graph one class at a time using the superclass link. Here is a possible description of the lookup algorithm that will be used for both instance and class methods.

```
lookup (selector class receiver):
    if the method is found in class
        then return it
        else if class == Object
            then send the message error to the receiver
            else lookup (selector superclass(class) receiver)
```

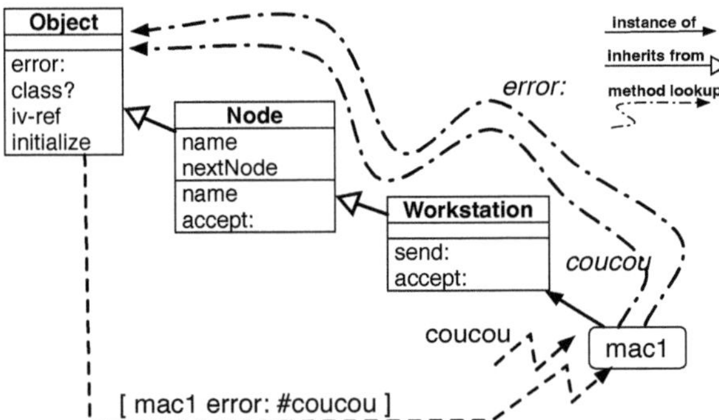

Figure 2-9 When a message is not found, another message is sent to the receiver supporting reflective operation.

2.7   Handling unknown messages

When the method is not found, the message `error` is sent as shown in Figure 2-9. Sending a message instead of simply reporting an error using a trace or an exception is a key design decision. In Pharo, this is done via the `doesNotUnderstand:` message, and it is an important reflective hook. Indeed classes can define their own implementation of the method `error` and perform specific actions to the case of messages that are not understood. For example, it is possible to implement proxies (objects representing other remote objects) or compile code on the fly by redefining such a message locally.

Now it should be noted that the previous algorithm has a limitation when a missing method has an arbitrary number of arguments. They are not passed to the `error` message. A better way to handle this is to decompose the algorithm differently as follows:

```
lookup (selector class):
   if the method is found in class
      then return it
      else if class == Object
            then return nil
            else lookup (selector superclass(class))
```

And then we redefined sending a message as follows:

```
sending a message (receiver argument)
   methodOrNil = lookup (selector classof(receiver)).
   if methodOrNil is nil
      then send the message error to the receiver
      else return apply(methodOrNil receiver arguments)
```

Remarks

This lookup is conceptually the same as in Pharo where all methods are public and virtual. There are no statically bound methods; even class methods are looked up dynamically. This allows for defining very elegant and dynamic registration mechanisms.

While the lookup happens at runtime, it is often cached. Languages usually have several systems of caches, e.g., global (class, selector), one per call site, etc.

2.8   Inheritance

In this kernel, there are two aspects of inheritance to consider:

- One static for the case where subclasses get superclass state. This instance variable inheritance is static in the sense that it happens only once at class creation time, i.e., at compilation time.

- One dynamic for behavior where methods are looked up during program execution. In this case, the inheritance tree is walked at run time.

Let's look at these two aspects.

Instance variable inheritance

Instance variable inheritance is done at class creation time. From that perspective, it is static and performed once. When a class C is created, its instance variables are the union of the instance variables of its superclass and the instance variables defined locally in class C. Each language defines the exact semantics of instance variable inheritance, for example, if they accept instance variables with the same name or not. In our model, we decide to use the simplest way: there should be no duplicate names.

```
instance-variables(aClass) =
  union (instance-variables(superclass(aClass)),
    local-instance-variables(aClass))
```

A word about the union of instance variables: when the implementation of the language is based on offsets to access instance variables, the union should make sure that the locations of inherited instance variables are kept ordered compared to the superclass. In general, we want to be able to apply methods of the superclass to subclasses without copying them down and recompiling them. Indeed if a method uses a variable at a given position in the instance variable lists, applying this method to instances of subclasses should work. In the implementation proposed next chapter, we will use accessors and will not support direct access to instance variables from a method body.

Method lookup

As previously described in Section 2.6, methods are looked up at runtime. Methods defined in superclasses are reused and applied to instances of subclasses. Contrary to instance variable inheritance, this part of inheritance is dynamic, i.e., it happens during program execution.

2.9   Object: defining the minimal behavior of any object

Object represents the minimal behavior that any object should understand, e.g., returning the class of the object, being able to handle errors, and initializing the object. This is why Object is the root of the hierarchy. Depending on the language, `Object` can be complex. In our kernel it is kept minimal as we will show in the implementation chapter.

Figure 2-10 shows the inheritance graph without the presence of instantiation. A Workstation is an object (i.e., it should at least understand the minimal behavior), so the class `Workstation` inherits directly or indirectly from the class `Object`. A class is also an object (i.e., it should understand the minimal behavior) so the class `Class` inherits from the class `Object`. In particular, the `class` (note the lowercase) instance variable is inherited from `Object` class.

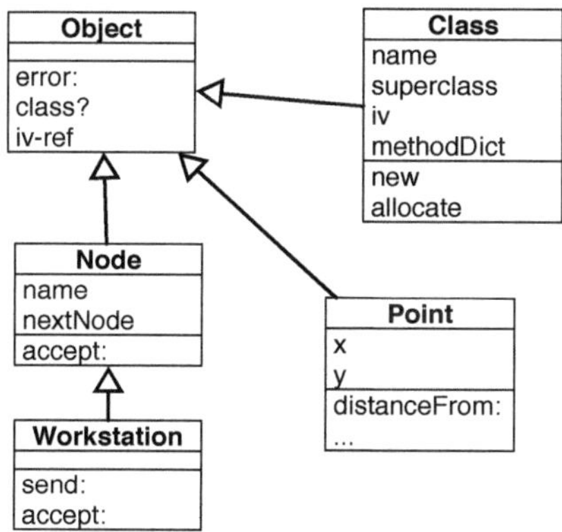

Figure 2-10 Full inheritance graph: Every class ultimately inherits from `Object`.

Remark

In Pharo, the class `Object` is not the root of inheritance. The root is in fact `ProtoObject`, and `Object` inherits from it. Most of the classes still inherit from `Object`. The design goal of `ProtoObject` is special: It supports the maximum generation of errors. Such errors can be captured via redefinition of the message `doesNotUnderstand:` and can support different scenarios such as implementing proxies.

2.10   Inheritance and instantiation together

Now that we have seen the instantiation and the inheritance graphs, we can examine the complete picture. Figure 2-11 shows the graphs and in particular how such graphs are used during message resolution:

- the instantiation link is used to find the starting class to look for any methods associated with the received message.

- the inheritance link is used to find inherited methods.

This process is the same when we send messages to the classes themselves. There is no difference between sending a message to an object or a class. The system *always* performs the same steps.

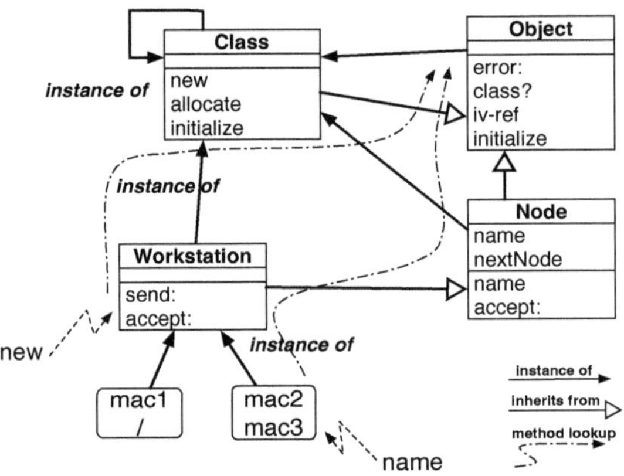

Figure 2-11 Kernel with instantiation and inheritance link.

2.11 Review of self and super semantics

Since our experience showed us that even some book authors got the essential semantics of object-oriented programming wrong, we review here some facts that programmers familiar with object-oriented programming should master. For further readings refer to *Pharo By Example* or the Pharo Mooc available at http://mooc.pharo.org.

As explained in Section 2.6, sending a message to an object always starts the lookup the corresponding method in the class of the receiver.

Now we should distinguish two cases: `self` and `super`. In the body of a method, both `self` (also called `this` in languages like Java) and `super` always represent the receiver of the message. Yes you read it well, both `self` and `super` always represent the receiver!

The difference lies in the class from where the lookup starts:

- For **self.** When a message is sent to `self`, the lookup of the method to execute starts in the class of the receiver.

When a message is sent to `super`, the lookup starts in the superclass of the method's class.

- For **super**. When a message is sent to super, the method lookup starts in the superclass of the class containing the super expression.

This distinction between **self** and **super** is required to handle the case where a method is redefined locally in a class but that you need to invoke the behavior defined in its superclasses. Note that the superclass method may be defined not in a direct superclass but one of the class ancestor, so there is a need for a method lookup and this method lookup should start above the method redefined it (here the method containing the **super** expression). Hence the name **super**.

Note that the lookup of a method in the case of super does not look in the superclass of the class of the receiver, since this would mean that it may loop forever in the case of inheritance tree with three classes.

Looking at Figure 2-12 we see that the key point is that B new bar returns 50 since the method is dynamically looked up and self represents the receiver, i.e., the instance of the class B. What is important to see is that sendings of self act as a hook and that subclasses' code can be injected in superclass code.

```
A new foo
>>> 10
B new foo
>>> 50
A new bar
>>> 10
B new bar
>>> 50
```

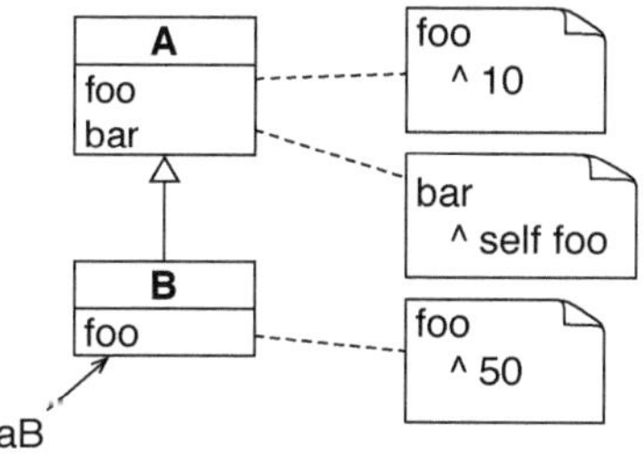

Figure 2-12   self always represents the receiver.

For super, the situation depicted in Figure 2-14 shows that super represents the receiver, but that when super is the receiver of a message, the method is looked up differently (starting from the superclass of the class using super) hence R new bar returns 100, but neither 20 nor 60.

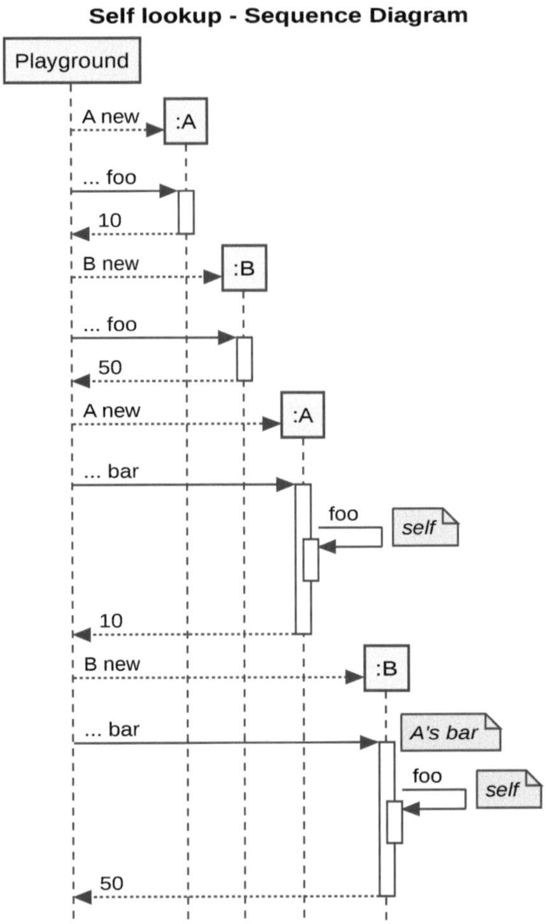

Figure 2-13 Sequence diagram of self always represents the receiver.

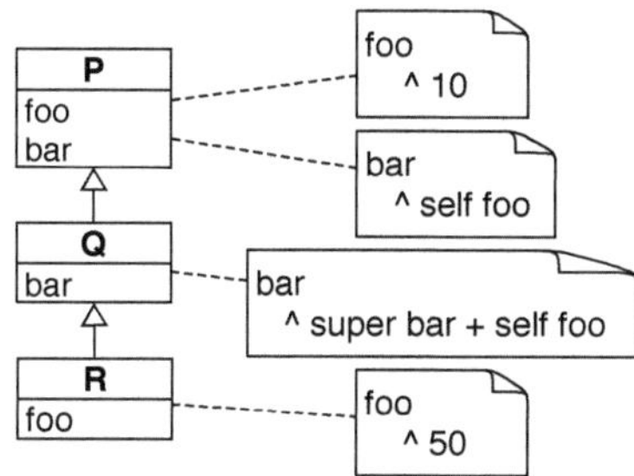

Figure 2-14   super represents the receiver, but the method lookup starts in the superclass of the class of the method using super.

```
Q new bar
>>> 20
R new bar
>>> 100
```

As a conclusion, we can say that self is dynamic and super static. Let us explain this view:

- When sending a message to self the lookup of the method begins in the class of the receiver. self is bound at execution-time. We do not know its value until execution time.

- super is static in the sense that while the object it will point to is only known at execution time, the place to look for the method is known at compile time: it should start to look in the class above the one containing super.

2.12   Object creation

Now we are ready to understand the creation of objects. In this model, there is only one way to create instances: we should send the message new to the class with a specification of the instance variable values as arguments.

2.13   Creation of instances of the class Point

The following examples show several point instantiations. What we see is that the model inherits from the Lisp tradition of passing arguments using keys and values, and that the order of arguments is not important.

```
Point new :x 24 :y 6
>>> aPoint (24 6)
Point new :y 6 :x 24
>>> aPoint (24 6)
```

When there is no value specified, the value of an instance variable is initialized to nil. It is worth to see that in CLOS (Common Lisp Object System) [7] provides the notion of default values for instance variable initialization. It can be added to ObjVlisp as an exercise and does not bring conceptual difficulties.

```
Point new
>>> aPoint (nil nil)
```

When the same argument is passed multiple times, then the implementation takes the first occurrence.

```
Point new :y 10 :y 15
>>> aPoint (nil 10)
```

We should not worry too much about such details: The point is that we can pass multiple arguments with a tag to identify them.

2.14 Creation of the class Point instance of Class

Since the class Point is an instance of the class Class, to create it, we should send the message new to the class as follows:

```
Class new
   :name 'Point'
   :superclass 'Object'
   :iv #(x y)
>>> aClass
```

What is interesting to see here is that we use exactly the same way to create an instance of the class Point as the class itself. Note that the possibility of having the same way to create objects or classes is also due to the fact that the arguments are specified using a list of pairs.

An implementation could have two different messages to create instances and classes. As soon as the same new, allocate, or initialize methods are involved, the essence of the object creation is similar and uniform.

Instance creation: Role of the metaclass

The following diagram (Figure 2-15) shows that despite what one might expect when we create a terminal instance the metaclass Class is involved in the process. Indeed, we send the message new to the class, to resolve this message, the system will look for the method in the class of the receiver (here Worksta-tion) which is the metaclass Class. The method new is found in the metaclass and applied to the receiver, the class Workstation. Its effect is to create an instance of the class Workstation.

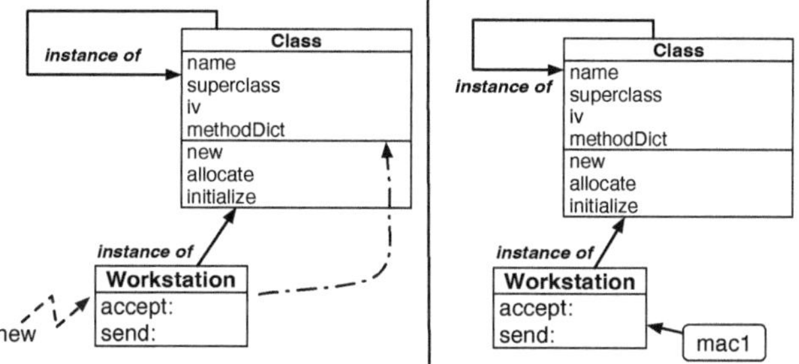

Figure 2-15   Metaclass role during instance creation: Applying plain message reso-lution. Right: situation before - Left: situation after the instance creation.

The same happens when creating a class. Figure 2-16 shows the process. We send a message, now this time, to the class Class. The system makes no ex-ception and to resolve the message, it looks for the method in the class of the receiver. The class of the receiver is itself, so the method new found in Class is applied to Class (the receiver of the message), and a new class is created.

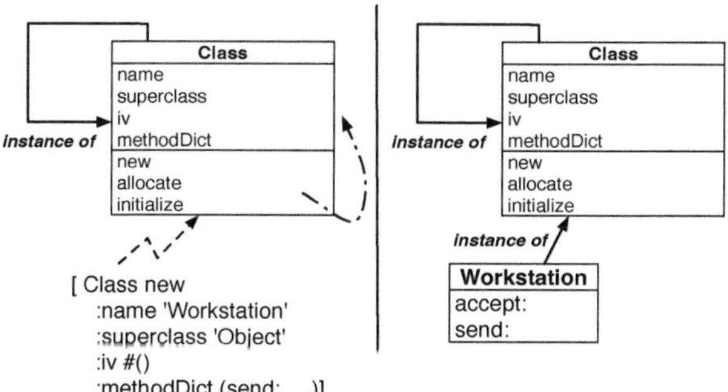

Figure 2-16   Metaclass role during class creation: Applying plain message resolu-tion - the self instantiation link is followed.

new = allocate and initialize

Creating an instance is the composition of two actions: a memory allocation allocate message and an object initialization message initialize.

In Pharo syntax, it means:

```
aClass new: args = (aClass allocate) initialize: args
```

We should see the following:

- The message new is a message sent to a class. The method new is a class method.
- The message allocate is a message sent to a class. The method allocate is a class method.
- The message initialize: will be executed on any newly created instance. If it is sent to a class, a class initialize: method will be invoked. If it is sent to a terminal object, an instance initialize: method will be executed (defined in Object).

Object allocation: the message allocate

Allocating an object means allocating enough space to the object state but there's more: instances should be marked with their class name or id. There is an invariant in this model and in general in object-oriented programming models. Every single object must have an identifier to its class, else the system will break when trying to resolve a message.

Object allocation should return a newly created instance with:

- empty instance variables (pointing to nil for example);
- an identifier to its class.

In the ObjVLisp model, the marking of an object as an instance of a class is performed by setting the value of the instance variable class inherited from Object. In Pharo, this information is not recorded as an instance variable but encoded in the internal object representation in the virtual machine.

The allocate method is defined on the metaclass Class. Here are some examples of allocation.

```
Point allocate
>>> #(Point nil nil)
```

A point allocation allocates three slots: one for the class and two for x and y values.

```
Class allocate
>>> #(Class nil nil nil nil nil)
```

The allocation for an object representing a class allocates six slots: one for class and one for each of the class instance variables: name, super, iv, keywords (see below), and methodDict.

Object initialization

Object initialization is the process of passing arguments as key/value pairs and assigning the value(s) to the corresponding instance variable(s).

This is illustrated in the following snippet. An instance of class `Point` is created and the key/value pairs (:y 6) and (:x 24) are specified. In the following snippet :y and :x are keywords in ObjVLisp parlance. They are built automatically from the instance variables and are used to uniquely identify values.

In the following snippet, the instance is created and it receives the `initialize:` message with the key/value pairs. The `initialize:` method is responsible for setting the corresponding variables in the receiver.

```
Point new :y 6  :x 24
>>> #(Point nil nil) initialize: (:y 6 :x 24)]
>>> #(Point 24 6)
```

When an object is initialized as a terminal instance, two actions are performed:

- First, we should get the values specified during the creation, i.e., get that the y value is 6 and the x value is 24,

- Second, we should assign the values to the corresponding instance variables of the created object.

Class initialization

During its initialization, a class should perform several steps:

- First, as with any initialization it should get the arguments and assign them to their corresponding instance variables. This is basically implemented by invoking the `initialize` method of `Object` via a super call, since `Object` is the superclass of `Class`.

- Second the inheritance of instance variables should be performed. Before this step, the class iv instance variable just contains the instance variables that are locally defined. After this step, the instance variable iv will contain all the instance variables inherited and local. In particular, this is where the `class` instance variable inherited from `Object` is added to the instance variables list of the subclass of `Object`.

- Third the class should be declared as a class pool or namespace so that programmers can access it via its name.

2.15 The Class class

Now we get a better understanding of what is the class `Class`:

- It is the initial metaclass and initial class.
- It defines the behavior of all the metaclasses.
- It defines the behavior of all the classes.

In particular, metaclasses define three messages related to instance creation.

- The new message, which creates an initialized instance of the class. It allocates the instance using the class message `allocate` and then initializes it by sending the message `initialize:` to this instance.
- The `allocate` message. Like the message new, it is a class message. It allocates the structure for the newly created object.
- Finally the message `initialize:`. This message has two definitions, one on `Object` and one on `Class`.

There is a difference between the method `initialize:` executed on any instance creation and the class `initialize:` method only executed when the created instance is a class.

- The first one is a method defined on the class of the object and potentially inherited from `Object`. This `initialize:` method just extracts the values corresponding to each instance variable from the argument list and sets them in the corresponding instance variables.
- The class `initialize:` method is executed when a new instance representing a class is executed. The message `initialize:` is sent to the newly created object but its specialization for classes will be found during method lookup and it will be executed. Usually, this method invokes the default ones, because the class parameter should be extracted from the argument list and set in their corresponding instance variables. But in addition, instance variable inheritance and class declaration in the class namespace is performed.

2.16 Conclusion

At this stage you saw all the concepts of this minimal object-oriented kernel where classes are themselves instances of other classes. In the following chapter, we explore more metaclasses and we encourage you to read it because it will shed an interesting light on the model.

CHAPTER 3

First metaclasses

In this chapter, we will study how all the concepts explained in the previous chapter fit together to let us define powerful metaclasses. Studying such entities will reinforce your understanding of the instantiation and inheritance relationships as well as their interplay. At the end of the chapter, we will explain why the sixth predicate of ObjVLisp is wrong and propose a solution that elegantly fits the model.

3.1 Defining a new Metaclass

Now we can study how we can add new metaclasses and see how the system handles them. To create a new metaclass is simple; it is enough to inherit from an existing one. Maybe this is obvious to you, but this is what we will check now.

Abstract

Imagine that we want to define abstract classes. We state that a class is abstract if it cannot create instances. To control the creation of instances of a class, we should define a new metaclass that forbids it. Therefore we will define a metaclass whose instances (abstract classes) cannot create instances.

We create a new metaclass named `AbstractMetaclass` which inherits from `Class` and we redefine the method `new` in this metaclass to raise an error (as shown in Figure 3-1). The following code snippet defines this new metaclass.

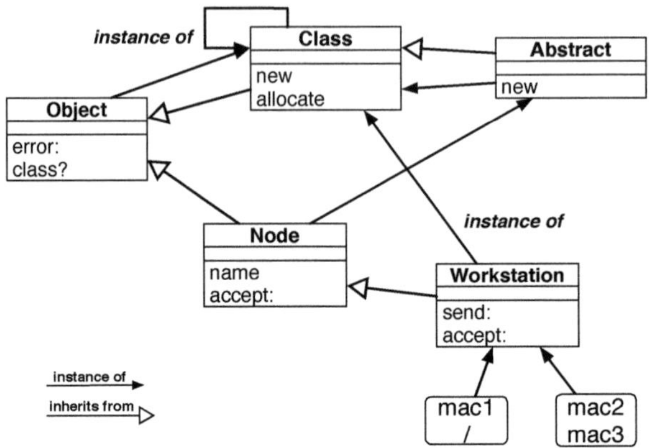

Figure 3-1   Abstract metaclass: its instance (i.e., the class Node) is abstract.

```
Class new
  :name 'AbstractMetaclass'
  :superclass 'Class'

AbstractMetaclass
  addMethod: #new
  body: [ :receiver :initargs | receiver error: 'Cannot create
    instance of class' ]
```

Two facts describe the relations between this metaclass and the class Class:

- AbstractMetaclass is a class, an instance of Class.

- AbstractMetaclass defines class behavior: It inherits from Class.

Now we can define an abstract class Node in ObjVLisp syntax:

```
AbstractMetaclass new
  :name 'Node'
  :super 'Object'
```

Sending a message new to the class Node will raise an error.

```
Node new
>>> Cannot create instance of class
```

A subclass of Node, for example, Workstation, can be a concrete class by being an instance of Class instead of AbstractMetaclass but still inheriting from Node. What we see in Figure 3-2 is that there are two links, instantiation and inheritance. The method lookup follows them as we presented previously. It always starts in the class of the receiver and follows the inheritance path.

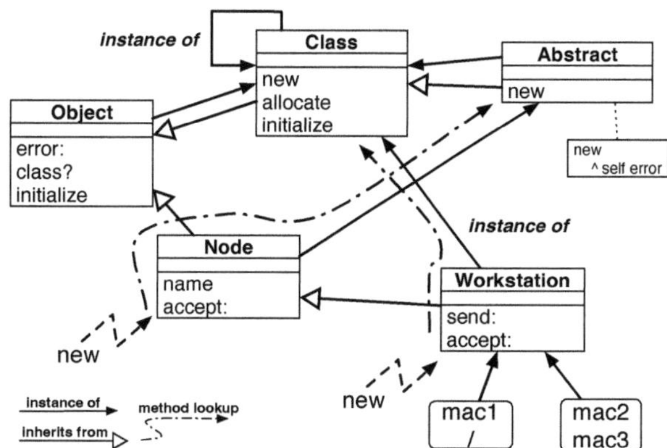

Figure 3-2 Abstract metaclass at work: Using message passing as a key to navigate the graph.

What is key to understand is that when we send the message `new` to the class `Workstation`, we look for methods first in the metaclass `Class`. When we send the message `new` to class `Node`, we look in its class: `AbstractMetaclass` as shown in Figure 3-2. In fact we do what we do for any instances: we look at the class of the receiver.

A class method is just implemented and follows the same semantics as instance methods: Sending the message `error` to the class `Node` starts in `Abstract-Metaclass`. Since we did not redefine it locally and it is not found there, the lookup will continue in the superclass of `AbstractClass`: the class `Class` and then the superclass of class `Class`, the class `Object`.

3.2 **About class state**

Imagine that we define a metaclass `WithSingleton` whose instances are classes that will have a unique instance. The situation is described in Figure 3-3. The class `WithSingleton` inherits from `Class` since it wants to reuse all of the class mechanisms. It is also an instance of class `Class`, since `WithSingleton` is a class and it can create instances. The class `Node` is an instance of class `With-Singleton`. When it receives the message `new`, the method `new` defined in the class `WithSingleton` is executed. If the unique instance variable is nil, it invokes the behavior defined in `Class` and stores it in the unique instance variable, and returns it.

Several questions still should be asked and answered.

- What is the instance variable list for the `WithSingleton` metaclass?

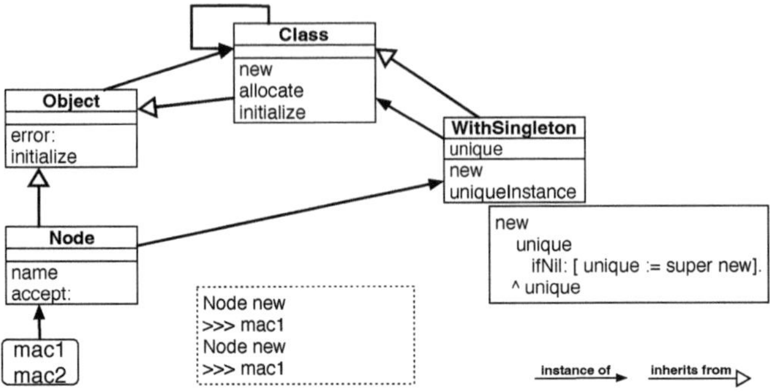

Figure 3-3   A WithSingleton metaclass: its instances can only have one instance.

- Where is the unique instance of the class Node or Process actually stored?

Instance variable of WithSingleton

As with any class, a subclass gets its instance variables as well as the instance variables of its superclass. Hence WithSingleton instance variables are the same as the one of Class, and it also has unique instance variable as shown in Fig. 3-4.

```
Singleton objIVs
>>> #(class name superclass iv keywords methodDict unique)
```

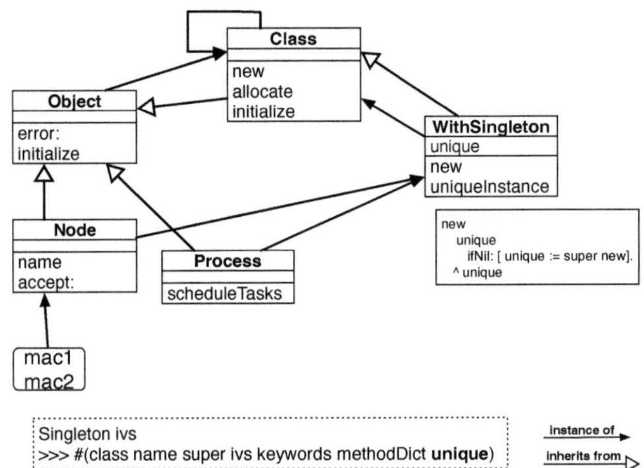

Figure 3-4   Storing unique instance.

Where is the singleton stored?

Each class instance of `WithSingleton` will have an additional value after its method dictionary. This is where the actual singleton of the class is stored. The class `Node` and `Process` are instances of the metaclass `WithSingleton`. Therefore they have one extra field in their structure to hold the unique instance variable values. Each instance of `WithSingleton` will have its own value: the instance of class playing the singleton role.

3.3 About the 6th postulate

As mentioned at the start of this chapter, the 6th postulate of ObjVLisp is wrong. Let us read it again:

"If the instance variables owned by an object define a local environment, there are also class variables defining a global environment shared by all the instances of a same class. These class variables are defined at the metaclass level according to the following equation: class variable [an-object] = instance variable [an-object's class]."

This says that class instance variables are equivalent to shared variables between instances, and this is wrong. Let us study this. According to the 6th postulate, a shared variable between instances is equal to an instance variable of the class. The definition is not totally clear so let us look at an example given in the article.

Illustrating the problem

Imagine that we would like the constant character '*' to be a class variable shared by all the points of the same class. We redefine the `Point` class as before, but metaclass of which (let us call it `MetaPoint`) specifies this common character For example, if a point has a shared variable named `char`, this instance variable should be defined in the class of the class `Point` called `Meta-Point`. The author proposes to define a new metaclass `MetaPoint` to hold a new instance variable to represent a shared variable between points.

```
Class new
  :name 'MetaPoint'
  :superclass 'Class'
  :iv #(char)
```

Then he proposes to use it as follows:

```
MetaPoint new
  :name Point
  :superclass 'Object'
  :iv #(x y)
  :char '*'
```

The class `Point` can define a method that accesses the character just by going to the class level. So why is this approach is wrong? Because it mixes levels. The instance variable `char` is not class information. It describes the terminal instances and not the instance of the metaclass. Why would the *metaclass* `MetaPoint` need a `char` instance variable?

The solution

The solution is that the shared variable `char` should be held in a list of the shared variables of the class `Point`. Any point instance can access this variable. The implication is that a *class* should have extra information to describe it. That is, an instance variable `sharedVariable` holding pairs, i.e., variable and its value. We should then be able to write:

```
Class new
   :name Point
   :superclass 'Object'
   :iv #(x y)
   :sharedivs {#char -> '*'}
```

Therefore the metaclass `Class` should get an extra instance variable named `sharedivs`, and each of its instances (the classes `Point`, `Node`, `Object`) can have different *values*. Such values can be shared among their instances by the compiler.

What we see is that `sharedivs` is from the `Class` vocabulary and we do not need an extra metaclass each time we want to share a variable. This design is similar to the one of Pharo where a class has a classVariable instance variable holding variables shared in all the subclasses of the class defining it.

3.4 Conclusion

We presented a small kernel composed of two classes: `Object`, the root of the inheritance tree, and `Class`, the first metaclass root of the instantiation tree. We revisited all the key points related to method lookup, object and class creation, and initialization. In the subsequent chapter, we propose to you how to implement such a kernel.

Further readings

The kernel presented in this chapter is a kernel with explicit metaclasses and as such it is not a panacea. Indeed it results in problems with metaclass composition as explained in Bouraqadi et al.'s excellent article.

CHAPTER 4

Getting started with the implementation

During the previous chapters, you saw the main conceptual points of the ObjVLisp model, now you will implement it. The objective of this chapter is to help you to implement step by step the model. To do so, we offer a skeleton of the implementation where key method bodies have been removed and replaced with an indication that you should implement them. In addition, a set of tests specifies the methods that are missing and that you should implement. Making the tests pass will guide you during your implementation.

4.1 Preparation

In this section, we discuss the setup that you will use, the implementation choices, and the conventions that we will follow during the rest of this book.

Getting Pharo 11

You need to download and install Pharo from http://www.pharo.org/. You need a virtual machine, and a couple image and changes. The best way is to use the PharoLauncher that is available at http://www.pharo.org/download.

You can also use http://get.pharo.org to get a script to download Pharo.

The current version of this book is working with Pharo 11.0.

```
wget -O- get.pharo.org/110+vm | bash
```

You can use the book *Pharo by Example* from http://www.pharo.org/PharoByEx-ample/ for an overview of the syntax and the system.

Getting infrastructure definitions

All the necessary method or class definitions are provided as a package. It contains all the classes, the method categories, and the method signatures of the methods that you have to implement. It provides additional functionality that will make your life easy and help you to concentrate on the essence of the model. It contains also all the tests of the functionality you have to implement.

To load the code, execute the following expression:

```
Metacello new
   baseline: 'ObjV';
   repository: 'github://Ducasse/ObjVLispSkeleton/tree/master/src';
   load
```

Running tests

For each functionality, you will have to run some tests.

For example to run a particular test named `testPrimitiveStructure`,

- evaluate the expression (`ObjTest run: #testPrimitiveStructure`), or

- click on the icon of the method named `testPrimitiveStructure`.

4.2 Naming conventions

We use the following conventions: we name as *primitives* all the Pharo methods that are used to build ObjVLisp. These primitives are mainly implemented as methods of the class `Obj`. Note that in a Lisp implementation, such primitives would be just lambda expressions, in a C implementation such primitives would be represented by C functions.

We also talk about *objInstances*, *objObjects*, and *objClasses* to refer to specific instances, objects, or classes defined in ObjVLisp.

To help you to distinguish between classes in the implementation language (Pharo) and the ObjVLisp model, we prefix all the ObjVLisp classes by `Obj`. Finally, some of the crucial and confusing primitives (mainly the class structure ones) are all prefixed by `obj`.

For example, the primitive that given an *objInstance* returns its class identifier is named `objClassId`.

4.3   Helping develop the kernel

To help you implement step by step the kernel of ObjVLisp, we defined tests that you will be able to execute one by one for each new aspect of ObjVLisp that you will define.

The problem is that to run a test, the kernel should be fully finished and we are defining it step by step. So we are trapped. Now to make sure that you can execute tests as soon as you define a method, we implemented *manually* some mocks of the objects that represent instances and classes in the ObjVLisp world: we basically created arrays and stuffed them with the correct information to mimick what the kernel once created will do. If you look at the methods `setUp` of the test classes you will see how we created them. Now pay attention because the setups are often taking shortcuts, so do not copy them blindly.

Finally, if you want to interact with objects during your development, for example to check manually that a pharo method is working or to explore your objClasses you can simply define a test method and put a breakpoint using `self halt`. When you execute this test, it will open a debugger and you will be able to execute code. For example the class `RawObjectTest` has several instances holding objects representing: the objClass `Object`, an objInstance of the objClass `Point`, the objClass `Point`.... Check the instance variables of the class `RawObjectTest`.

Figure 4-1 shows a method named `testBidouille` with a halt. It also shows that we can interact and send messages to the objects that were manually created. Here we executed the primitive `objName` on the objClass `pointClass` and it returned #ObjPoint.

4.4   Inheriting from class Array

We do not want to implement a scanner, a parser, and a compiler for ObjVLisp but concentrate on the essence of the language. That's why we chose to use as much as possible the implementation language, here Pharo. In our implementation, every object in the ObjVLisp world is an instance of the class `Obj`. The class `Obj` is a subclass of `Array`.

Since the Pharo class `Obj` is a subclass of the Pharo class `Array`, the following array #(#ObjPoint 10 15) represents an objInstance of the objClass `Obj-Point`. From an implementation point of view, this objClass `ObjPoint` is just an instance of the Pharo class `Obj`.

As we will see:

- #(#ObjPoint 10 15) represents an objPoint (10,15). It is an objInstance of the objClass `ObjPoint`.

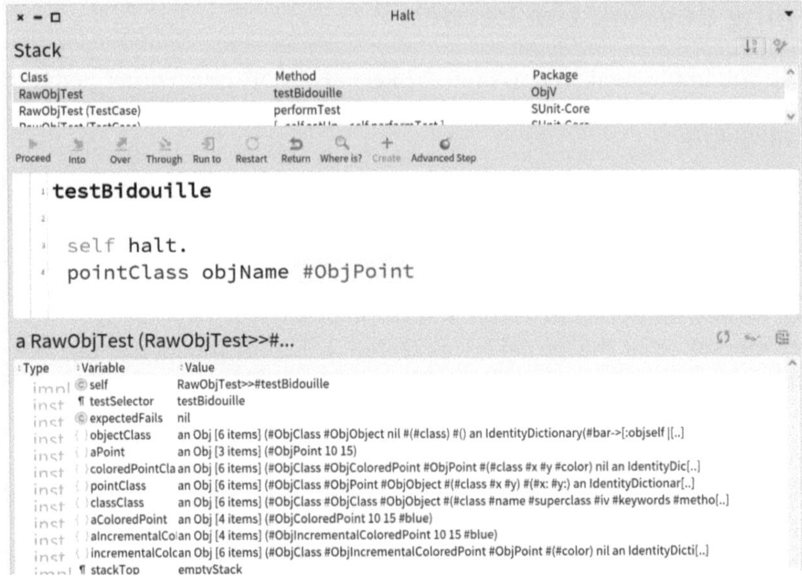

Figure 4-1 Interacting in the debugger with some objinstances.

- #(#ObjClass #ObjPoint #ObjObject #(class x y) #(:x :y) nil
) is the array that represents the objClass ObjPoint.

4.5 Facilitating objClass class access

In the previous chapter, we wrote some expressions using some objClass such as `ObjPoint objIVs` that returns the instance variables of the objClass `Obj-Point`.

If you simply execute this expression in Pharo you will get an error. Indeed, the objClass `ObjPoint` is not a Pharo class and it is not known to Pharo: It is not added to the Pharo namespace and this is normal because it is another world.

The question is then how can we provide simple access to objClasses once they are created. For this, we need a way to store and access ObjVLisp classes. As a solution, on the *class* level of the Pharo class `Obj`, we defined a dictionary holding the defined classes. The keys of this dictionary are the objClass names and the values are the objClasses with the corresponding name. This dictionary acts as the namespace for our language. We defined the following methods to store and access defined classes.

- `declareClass: anObjClass` stores the objInstance anObjClass given as an argument in the class repository (here a dictionary whose keys are the class names and values the ObjVLisp classes themselves).

- `giveClassNamed:` `aSymbol` returns the ObjVLisp class named `aSymbol` if it exists. The class should have been declared previously.

With such methods, we can write code like the following: Here we get access to the objClass `ObjPoint`.

```
Obj giveClassNamed: #ObjPoint
>>> #(#ObjClass 'ObjPoint' #ObjObject #(class x y) #(:x :y) ... )
```

Then we can access some of its state. For example we access the instance variables of the class as follows:

```
(Obj giveClassNamed: #ObjPoint) objIVs
>>>  #(class x y)
```

To make class access less heavy, we also implemented a shortcut: We trap messages not understood sent to `Obj` and look into the defined class dictionary. Since `ObjPoint` is an unknown message, this same code is then written as:

```
Obj ObjPoint
>>> #(#ObjClass 'ObjPoint' #ObjObject #(class x y) #(:x :y) ... )
```

Now you are ready to start.

CHAPTER 5

Primitives for a reflective class-based kernel

Now that all the infrastructure has been explained you are ready to start. The first tasks are to define how we will manipulate objObjects. We will define Pharo methods that will act as primitive functionalities to build later the language kernel. Such primitives could be written in C, assembly or any other languages. They are the low-level functionalities on top of which we will build the object model of ObjVLisp: mainly the class ObjObject and ObjClass.

5.1 Structure and primitives

The first issue is how to represent objects. We have to agree on an initial representation. In this implementation, we chose to represent the objInstances as arrays (instances of Obj a subclass of Array). In the following, we use the term 'array' for talking about instances of the class Obj.

Your job.

Check that the class Obj exists and inherits from Array.

5.2 Structure of a class

The first object that we will have to create is the class ObjClass. Therefore we focus now on the minimal structure of the classes in our language.

An objInstance representing a class has the following structure: an identifier to its class, a name, an identifier to its superclass (we limit the model to single inheritance), a list of instance variables, a list of initialization keywords, and a method dictionary.

For example, the class `ObjPoint` has the following structure:

```
#(#ObjClass #ObjPoint #ObjObject #(class x y) #(:x :y) nil)
```

It means that the objClass `ObjPoint` is an instance of `ObjClass`, is named `#ObjPoint`, inherits from a class named `ObjObject`, has three instance variables, two initialization keywords, and an uninitialized method dictionary. To access this structure we define some primitives as shown in Figure 5-1.

```
#(
    #ObjClass        offsetForClassId (1)
    #ObjPoint        offsetForName (2)
    #ObjObject       offsetForSuperclassId (3)
    #(class x y)     offsetForIVs (4)
    #(:x :y)         offsetForKeywords (5)
    nil              offsetForMethodDict (6)
)
```

Figure 5-1 Class structure representation.

To avoid manipulating numbers we defined some Pharo methods returning the corresponding constants of the object and class structure. These methods start with the `offset` term. We have `offsetForClassIdId`, `offsetForName`, `offsetOfSuperclassId`, and more. Figure 5-2 shows how offsets are used to access the information of an objClass.

Here is the definition of `offsetForName`: It just defines that given an objobject representing an objclass the name of the class is located at the second position.

```
Obj >> offsetForName
  ^ 2
```

Using the method `offsetForName` we can simply define a Pharo primitive named `objName` that returns the name of a class as follows:

```
Obj >> objName
  ^ self at: self offsetForName
```

The corresponding setter `objName:` is then defined as follows:

```
Obj >> objName: aString
  ^ self at: self offsetForName put: aString
```

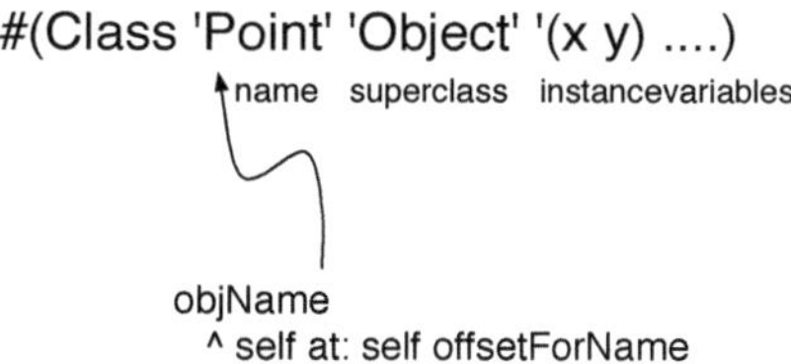

Figure 5-2   Using offset to access information.

Your job.

The test methods of the class `RawObjTest` that are in the categories `'step01-tests-structure of objects'` and `'step02-tests-structure of classes'` give some examples of structure accesses. Here are two examples of such test methods:

```
RawObjTest >> testPrimitiveStructureObjClassId
    self assert: pointClass objClassId equals: #ObjClass


RawObjTest >> testPrimitiveStructureObjIVs
    self assert: pointClass objIVs equals: #(#class #x #y)
```

Access of ClassId for any objects.

Using the method `offsetForClassIdId`, implement in protocol `'object structure primitives'` the primitives `objClassId` and `objClassId: aSymbol`. The receiver is an `objObject`. This means that this primitive can be applied on any objInstances (be it a class or an instance such as a point objObject) to get its class identifier. Execute the test method `testPrimitiveStructureObjClassId`.

Class structure access.

Now we can focus on the other primitives that give access to class information.

Implement in protocol `'class structure primitives'` the primitives that manage:

- the class name. Methods `objName` and `objName: aSymbol`. The receiver is an `objClass`. Execute test method `testPrimitiveStructureObjName`.

- the superclass. Methods `objSuperclassId` and `objSuperclassId: aSymbol`. The receiver is an `objClass`. Execute test method `testPrimitiveStructureObjSuperclassId`

- the instance variables. Methods `objIVs` and `objIVs: anOrderedCollection`. The receiver is an `objClass`. Execute test method `testPrimitiveStructureObjIVs`.

- the keyword list. Methods `objKeywords` and `objKeywords: anOrderedCollection`. The receiver is an `objClass`. Execute test method `testPrimitiveStructureObjKeywords`.

- the method dictionary. Methods `objMethodDict` and `objMethodDict: anIdentityDictionary`. The receiver is an `objClass`. Execute test method `testPrimitiveStructureObjMethodDict`.

5.3 Finding the class of an object

Every object keeps the identifier of its class (its name). For example, an instance of `ObjPoint` has then the following structure: `#(#ObjPoint 10 15)` where `#ObjPoint` is a symbol identifying the class `ObjPoint`.

Your job.

Using the primitive `giveClassNamed: aSymbol` defined at the class level of Obj (See Section 4.5), define the primitive `objClass` in the protocol `'object-structure primitive'` that returns the `objInstance` that represents its class (classes are objects too in ObjVLisp).

Make sure that you execute the test method: `testClassAccess`

```
RawObjTest >> testClassAccess
    self assert: aPoint objClass equals: pointClass
```

Now we will be ready to manipulate objInstances via proper API. We will now use the class `ObjTest` for more elaborate tests.

5.4 Accessing object instance variable values

A first simple method.

Now you will implement a primitive that when sent to an objClass returns the offset of the instance variable represented by the symbol. It returns 0 if the variable is not defined. The following test illustrates the behavior of this primitive `ivClassOffset:` (It could have been named `classOffsetForIV:`)

```
ObjTest >> testIVOffset
    self
     assert: (pointClass ivClassOffset: #x)
     equals: 2.
```

```
#(
    #ObjClass
    #ObjPoint
    #ObjObject
    #(class x y)   ivClassOffset: #x
    #(:x :y)
    nil
)                      >>> 2
```

Figure 5-3   Instance variable offset asked to the class.

```
self
  assert: (pointClass ivClassOffset: #lulu)
  equals: 0
```

Your job.

In the protocol `'iv management'` define a method called `ivClassOffset:`
`aSymbol` Look at the tests `#testIVOffset` of the class `ObjTest`. Make sure that
you execute the test method: `testIVOffset`.

Hints: Use the Pharo method `indexOf:`. Pay attention that such a primitive is
applied to an objClass as shown in the test.

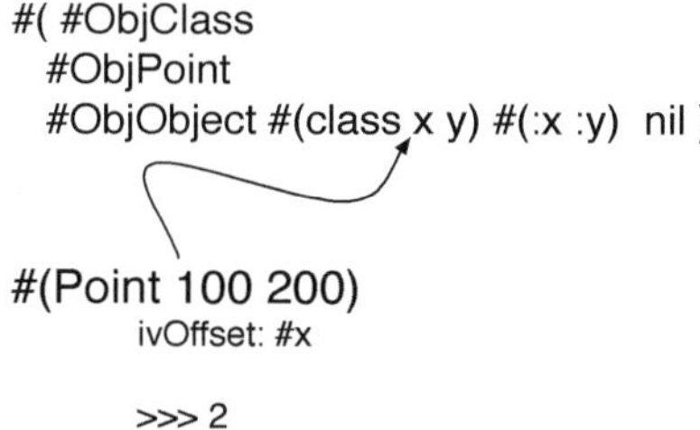

Figure 5-4   Instance variable offset asked to the instance itself.

Two simple methods.

Now that we know from the class the offset for a given instance variable, we
can define a primitive that performs a similar behavior but that is sent to an
instance and not a class. Using it we can easily get access to the value of an instance variable of an instance.

The following test illustrates the expected behavior:

```
ObjTest >> testIVOffsetAndValue

  self
    assert: (aPoint ivOffset: #x)
  equals: 2.
  self
    assert: (aPoint valueOfInstanceVariable: #x)
  equals: 10
```

Your job.

Using the previous method, define in the protocol `'iv management'`:

1. When sent to an objObject, the primitive `ivOffset: aSymbol` that returns the offset of the instance variable. Note that this time the method is applied to an objInstance presenting an instance and not a class (as shown in Figure 5-4). (It could have been named `objectOffsetForIV:`).

2. the method `valueOfInstanceVariable: aSymbol` that returns the value of this instance variable in the given object as shown in the test below.

Note that for the method `ivOffset:` you can check that the instance variable exists in the class of the object and else raise an error using the Pharo method `error:`.

Make sure that you execute the test method: `testIVOffsetAndValue` and it passes.

5.5   Object allocation and initialization

The creation of an object is the composition of two elementary operations: its *allocation* and its *initialization*. We now define the primitives that allow us to allocate and initialize an object. Remember that:

- allocation is a class method that returns a nearly empty structure, nearly empty because the instance represented by the structure should at least know its class, and

- initialization is an instance method that given a newly allocated instance and a list of initialization arguments fill the instance.

Instance allocation

As shown in the class `ObjTest`, if the class `ObjPoint` has two instance variables: `ObjPoint allocateAnInstance` returns `#(#ObjPoint nil nil)`.

```
ObjTest >> testAllocate

    | newInstance |
    newInstance := pointClass allocateAnInstance.
    self assert: (newInstance at: 1) equals: #ObjPoint.
    self assert: (newInstance size) equals: 3.
    self assert: (newInstance at: 2) isNil.
    self assert: (newInstance at: 3) isNil.
    self assert: newInstance objClass equals: pointClass
```

Your job.

In the protocol `'instance allocation'` implement the primitive called `allocateAnInstance` that when sent to an *objClass* returns a new instance whose instance variable values are nil and whose objClassId represents the objClass.

Hints: in Pharo we use the message `new:` to specify the size of Arrays. For example, `Array new: 5` will create an array of 5 elements.

Make sure that you execute the test method: `testAllocate`

5.6   Keywords primitives

The original implementation of ObjVLisp uses the facility offered by the Lisp keywords to ease the specification of the instance variable values during instance creation. It also provides a uniform and unique way to create objects. We have to implement some functionality to support keywords. However, as this is not really interesting that you lose time we give you all the necessary primitives.

Your job.

All the functionality for managing the keywords are defined in the protocol `'keyword management'`. Read the code and the associated test called `testKeywords` in the class `ObjTest`.

```
ObjTest >> testKeywords

    | dummyObject |
    dummyObject := Obj new.
    self
        assert: (dummyObject generateKeywords: #(#titi #toto #lulu))
```

```
        equals: #(#titi: #toto: #lulu:).
    self
        assert:
            (dummyObject
                keywordValue: #x
                getFrom: #(#toto 33 #x 23)
                ifAbsent: 2)
        equals: 23.
    self
        assert:
            (dummyObject
                keywordValue: #x
                getFrom: #(#toto 23)
                ifAbsent: 2)
        equals: 2.
    self
        assert:
            (dummyObject
                returnValuesFrom: #(#x 22 #y 35)
                followingSchema: #(#y #yy #x #y))
        equals: #(35 nil 22 35)
```

Make sure that you execute the test method: `testKeywords` and that it passes.

5.7 Object initialization

Once an object is allocated, it may be initialized by the programmer by specifying a list of initialization values. We can represent such a list by an array containing alternatively a keyword and a value like `#(#toto 33 #x 23)` where 33 is associated with `#toto` and 23 with `#x`.

Your job.

Read in the protocol `'instance initialization'` the primitive `initializeUsing: anArray` that, when sent to an object along with an initialization list, returns the initialized object.

```
ObjTest >> testInitialize

    | newInstance |
    newInstance := pointClass allocateAnInstance.
    newInstance initializeUsing: #(#y: 2 #z: 3 #t: 55 #x: 1).
    self assert: (newInstance at: 1) equals: #ObjPoint.
    self assert: (newInstance at: 2) equals: 1.
    self assert: (newInstance at: 3) equals: 2.
```

5.8   **Static inheritance of instance variables**

Instance variables are statically inherited at class creation time. The simplest
form of instance variable inheritance is to define the complete set of instance
variables as the *ordered fusion* between the inherited instance variables and
the locally defined instance variables. For simplicity and similarity with most
languages, we chose to forbid duplicated instance variables in the inheritance
chain.

Your job.

In the protocol `'iv inheritance'`, read and understand the primitive `com-
puteNewIVFrom: superIVOrdCol with: localIVOrdCol`.

The primitive takes two ordered collections of symbols and returns an ordered
collection containing the union of the two ordered collections but with the
extra constraint that the order of elements of the first ordered collection is
kept. Look at the test method `testInstanceVariableInheritance` below for
examples.

Make sure that you execute the test method: `testInstanceVariableInheri-
tance` and that it passes.

```
ObjTest >> testInstanceVariableInheritance
    "a better choice would be to throw an exception if there are
     duplicates"
    self
        assert:
        (Obj new
    computeNewIVFrom: #(#a #b #c #d)
    with: #(#a #z #b #t))
        equals: #(#a #b #c #d #z #t).
    self
        assert: (Obj new
      computeNewIVFrom: #()
      with: #(#a #z #b #t))
        equals: #(#a #z #b #t)
```

Side remark

You could think that keeping the same order of the instance variables between
a superclass and its subclass is not an issue. This is partly true in this simple
implementation because the instance variable accessors compute each time
the corresponding offset to access an instance variable using the primitive `iv-
ClassOffset:`. However, the structure (instance variable order) of a class is
hardcoded by the primitives. That's why your implementation of the primitive

`computeNewIVFrom:with:` should take care of that aspect. In real language, compilers will try to ensure that a method defined in a superclass can be applied to instances of the subclasses.

5.9 Method management

A class defines the instance behavior expressed by methods stored in a method dictionary. As such they are shared by all the instances of a class. In our implementation, we represent methods by associating a symbol to a Pharo *block* (a lexical closure). The block is then stored in the method dictionary of an objClass.

In this implementation, we do not offer the ability to directly access instance variables of the class in which the method is defined. This could be done by sharing a common environment among all the methods. The programmer has to use accessors or the `setIV` and `getIV` objMethods defined on `ObjObject` to access the instance variables. You can find the definition of those methods in the bootstrap protocol on the class side of `Obj`.

In our ObjVLisp implementation, we do not have a specific (non Pharo) syntax for message passing. Instead, we call the primitives using the Pharo syntax for message passing using the message `send:withArguments:`. The objVLisp expression `objself getIV: #x` is expressed as follows: `objself send: #getIV withArguments: #(#x)`.

Method definition.

We need a way to define a method, e.g., add a block to the method dictionary. We use the method `addUnaryMethod: aName withBody: aString`.

The following code describes the *definition* of the accessor method x defined on the objClass `ObjPoint` that invokes a field access using the message `getIV`.

```
ObjPoint
    addUnaryMethod: #x
    withBody: 'objself send: #getIV withArguments: #(#x)'.
```

As a first approximation, this code will create the following block that will get stored in the class method dictionary: `[ :objself | objself send: #getIV withArguments: #(#x) ]`. As you may notice, in our implementation, the receiver is always an explicit argument of the method. Here we named it objself.

We propose two variations for the method definition: The primitives `addUnaryMethod:withBody:` and `addMethod:args:withBody:`. The first one is a version that avoids having an empty list of arguments.

```
ObjPoint
    addMethod: #x
    args: ''
    withBody: 'objself send: #getIV withArguments: #(#x)'.
```

Note that the arguments of args: are expressed in a string where arguments
are separated by a space.

Defining a method and sending a message

As we want to keep this implementation as simple as possible, we define only
one primitive for sending a message: it is send:withArguments:. To see the
mapping between Pharo and ObjVlisp ways of expressing message sent, look at
the comparison below:

```
Pharo Unary: self odd
ObjVLisp: objself send: #odd withArguments: #()

Pharo Binary: a + 4
ObjVLisp: a send: #+ withArguments: #(4)

Pharo Keyword: a max: 4
ObjVLisp: a send: #max: withArguments: #(4)
```

While in Pharo you would write the following method definition:

```
bar: x
    self foo: x
```

In our implementation of ObjVlisp you write:

```
anObjClass
    addMethod: #bar:
    args: 'x'
    withBody: 'objself send: #foo: withArguments: #(x)'.
```

Your job.

We provide all the primitives that handle method definition.

- Read the methods addMethod: aSelector args: aString withBody:
  aStringBlock, removeMethod: aSelector, and doesUnderstand: aS-
  elector - they are grouped in the protocol 'method management'.

- Implement bodyOfMethod: aSelector.

Make sure that you execute the test method: testMethodManagement

```
ObjTest >> testMethodManagement

   self assert: (pointClass doesUnderstand: #x).
   self assert: (pointClass doesUnderstand: #xx) not.

   pointClass
      addUnaryMethod: #xx
      withBody: 'objself valueOfInstanceVariable: #x '.
   self assert: ((pointClass bodyOfMethod: #xx) value: aPoint) equals:
     10.
   self assert: (pointClass doesUnderstand: #xx).
   pointClass removeMethod: #xx.
   self assert: (pointClass doesUnderstand: #xx) not.
   self assert: ((pointClass bodyOfMethod: #x) value: aPoint) equals:
     10
```

5.10 Message passing and dynamic lookup

Sending a message is the result of the composition of *method lookup* and *execution*.

The following basicSend:withArguments:from: primitive just implements
it. First, it looks up the method into the class or superclass of the receiver then
if a method has been found it executes it, else lookup: returns nil and we raise
a Pharo error.

```
Obj >> basicSend: selector withArguments: arguments from: aClass
   "Execute the method found starting from aClass and whose name is
     selector.
   The core of message sending reused for both a normal send or a
     super one."

   | methodOrNil |
   methodOrNil := aClass lookup: selector.
   ^ methodOrNil
      ifNotNil: [ methodOrNil valueWithArguments: (Array with: self) ,
     arguments ]
      ifNil: [ Error signal: 'Obj message' , selector asString, ' not
     understood' ]
```

Based on this primitive we can express send:withArguments: as follows:

```
Obj >> send: selector withArguments: arguments
   "send the message whose selector is <selector> to the receiver. The
     arguments of the messages are an array <arguments>. The method is
     looked up in the class of the receiver. self is an objObject or a
     objClass."
```

```
^ self basicSend: selector withArguments: arguments from:  self
   objClass
```

Note that the definition above of basicSend:withArguments:from: does not
let us ObjVLisp developers redefine the error handing. We will propose a solution in subsequent sections.

5.11   Method lookup

The primitive lookup: selector applied to an objClass should return the
method associated to the selector if it found it, else nil to indicate that it failed.

Your job.

Implement the primitive lookup: selector that when sent to an objClass
with a method selector, a symbol, and the initial receiver of the message, returns the method-body of the method associated with the selector in the obj-
Class or its superclasses. Moreover, if the method is not found, nil is returned.

Make sure that you execute the test methods: testNilWhenErrorInLookup
and testRaisesErrorSendWhenErrorInLookup whose code is given below:

```
ObjTest >> testNilWhenErrorInLookup

   self assert: (pointClass lookup: #zork) isNil.
   "The method zork is NOT implemented on pointClass"
```
```
ObjTest >> testRaisesErrorSendWhenErrorInLookup

   self should: [ pointClass send: #zork withArguments: { aPoint } ]
      raise: Error.
```

5.12   Managing super

To invoke a superclass hidden method, in Java and Pharo you use super, which
means that the lookup up will start above the class defining the method containing the super expression. In fact, we can consider that in Java or Pharo, super is a syntactic sugar to refer to the receiver but changes where the method
lookup starts. This is what we see in our implementation where we do not have
syntactic support.

Let us see how we will express the following situation.

```
bar: x
   super foo: x
```

In our implementation of ObjVlisp we do not have a syntactic construct to express super, you have to use the `super:withArguments:from:` Pharo message as follows.

```
anObjClass
    addMethod: #bar:
    args: 'x'
    withBody: 'objself super: #foo: withArguments: #(#x) from:
      superclassOfClassDefiningTheMethod'.
```

Note that `superclassOfClassDefiningTheMethod` is a variable that is bound to the superclass of `anObjClass` i.e., the class defining the method `bar` (see later).

```
Pharo Unary: super odd
ObjVLisp: objself super: #odd withArguments: #() from:
    superclassOfClassDefiningTheMethod

Pharo Binary: super + 4
ObjVLisp: objself super: #+ withArguments: #(4) from:
    superclassOfClassDefiningTheMethod

Pharo Keyword: super max: 4
ObjVlisp: objself super: #max: withArguments: #(4) from:
    superclassOfClassDefiningTheMethod
```

5.13 Representing super

We would like to explain to you where the `superclassOfClassDefiningTheMethod` variable comes from. When we compare the primitive `send:withArguments:` to its variation using super, for super sends we added a third parameter to the primitive and we called it `super:withArguments:from:`.

This extra parameter corresponds to the superclass of the class in which the method is defined. This argument should always have the same name, i.e., `superclassOfClassDefiningTheMethod`. This variable will be set when the method is added to the method dictionary of an objClass.

If you want to understand how we bind the variable, here is the explanation: In fact, a method is not only a block but it needs to know the class that defines it or its superclass. We added such information using a currification. A currification is the transformation of a function with n arguments into function with less arguments but an environment capture: $f(x,y) = (+ x y)$ is transformed into a function $f(x)=f(y)(+ x y)$ that returns a function of a single argument y and where x is bound to a value and obtain a function generator. For example, $f(2,y)$ returns a function $f(y)=(+ 2 y)$ that adds its parameter to

2. A currification acts as a generator of functions where one of the arguments
of the original function is fixed.

In Pharo, we wrap the block representing the method around another block
with a single parameter and we bind this parameter with the superclass of the
class defining the method. When the method is added to the method dictionary, we evaluate the first block with the superclass as a parameter as illustrated as follows:

```
method := [ :superclassOfClassDefiningTheMethod |
      [ :objself :otherArgs  |
            ... method code ...
            ]]
method value: (Obj giveClassNamed: self objSuperclassId)
```

So now you know where the `superclassOfClassDefiningTheMethod` variable
comes from. Make sure that you execute the test method: `testMethodLookup`
and that i passes.

Your job.

Now you should implement `super: selector withArguments: arguments
from: aSuperclass` using the primitive `basicSend:withArguments:from:`.

5.14   Handling not understood messages

Now we can revisit error handling. Instead of raising a Pharo error, we want to
send an ObjVlisp message to the receiver of the message to give him a chance
to trap the error.

Compare the two following versions of `basicSend: selector withArguments: arguments from: aClass` and propose an implementation of `sendError: selector withArgs: arguments`.

```
Obj >> basicSend: selector withArguments: arguments from: aClass

   | methodOrNil |
   methodOrNil := (aClass lookup: selector).
   ^ methodOrNil
     ifNotNil: [ methodOrNil valueWithArguments: (Array with: self) ,
   arguments ]
     ifNil: [ Error signal: 'Obj message' , selector asString, ' not
   understood' ]
```

```
Obj >> basicSend: selector withArguments: arguments from: aClass

   | methodOrNil |
   methodOrNil := (aClass lookup: selector).
   ^ methodOrNil
      ifNotNil: [ methodOrNil valueWithArguments: (Array with: self) ,
     arguments ]
       ifNil: [ self sendError: selector withArgs: arguments ]
```

It should be noted that the obj method is defined as follows in the ObjObject class (see the bootstrap method on the class side of the class Obj). The obj error method expects a single parameter: an array of arguments whose first element is the selector of the not understood message.

```
objObject
   addMethod: #error
   args: 'arrayOfArguments'
   withBody: 'Transcript show: ''error '', arrayOfArguments first.
     ''error '', arrayOfArguments first'.
```

```
Obj >> sendError: selector withArgs: arguments
   "send error wrapping arguments into an array with the selector as
    first argument. Instead of an array we should create a message
    object."

   ^ self send: #error withArguments:  {(arguments copyWithFirst:
    selector)}
```

Make sure that you read and execute the test method: testSendErrorRaisesErrorSendWhenErrorInLookup. Have a look at the implementation of the #error method defined in ObjObject and in the assembleObjectClass of the ObjTest class.

6

Defining the language kernel

Now you have implemented all the primitives we need, you are ready to define the two classes that represent the ObjVLisp kernel: `ObjClass` and `ObjObject`. Once such classes will exist we will be able to code using ObjVLisp and not in Pharo anymore. The moment where we go from the low-level world (here Pharo) to the high-level one (here ObjVLisp) is generally called the bootstrap of the language. Indeed after this last phase, our new language exists.

To implement these two classes we could them by manipulating low-level primitives and doing all the plumbing ourselves as what we did in the test `setUp` methods. But there is something better to do. We can use the high level language to use itself to define itself. This is what we will explain in this chapter.

6.1 About bootstrap

to bootstrap the system: this means creating the kernel consisting of `ObjObject` and `ObjClass` classes from themselves. The idea of a smart bootstrap is to be as lazy as possible and to use the system to create itself by creating a fake but working first class with which we will build the rest.

Three steps compose the ObjVlisp bootstrap:

1. Create by hand the minimal part of the objClass `ObjClass` and then

2. Use it to create normally `ObjObject` objClass and then

3. Recreate normally and completely `ObjClass`.

These three steps are described by the following bootstrap method of `Obj` class.
Note the bootstrap is defined as class methods of the class `Obj`.

```
Obj class >> bootstrap
    "self bootstrap"

    self initialize.
    self manuallyCreateObjClass.
    self createObjObject.
    self createObjClass.
```

To help you to implement the functionality of the objClasses `ObjClass` and`ObjObject`,
we defined another set of tests in the class `ObjTestBootstrap`. Read them.

6.2   Manually creating ObjClass

The first step is to create manually the class `ObjClass`. By manually we mean
create an array (because we chose an array to represent instances and classes
in particular) that represents the objClass `ObjClass`, then define its methods.
You will implement/read this in the primitive `manuallyCreateObjClass` as
shown below:

```
Obj class >> manuallyCreateObjClass
   "self manuallyCreateObjClass"

   | class |
   class := self manualObjClassStructure.
   Obj declareClass: class.
   self defineManualInitializeMethodIn: class.
   self defineAllocateMethodIn: class.
   self defineNewMethodIn: class.
   ^ class
```

We will comment some of the methods called in `manuallyCreateObjClass`.

For this purpose, you have to implement/read all the primitives that compose
it.

Your job.

At the class level in the protocol `'bootstrap objClass manual'` read or implement: the primitive `manualObjClassStructure` that returns an objObject
that represents the class `ObjClass`.

Make sure that you execute the test method: `testManuallyCreateObjClassStruc-`
`ture`

- As the `initialize` of this first phase of the bootstrap is not easy we give you its code. Note that the definition of the objMethod `initialize` is done in the primitive method `defineManualInitializeMethodIn:`.

```
Obj class >> defineManualInitializeMethodIn: class

    class
     addMethod: #initialize
     args: 'initArray'
     withBody:
       '| objsuperclass |
       objself initializeUsing: initArray.  "Initialize a class as an
     object. In the bootstrapped system will be done via super"
       objsuperclass := Obj giveClassNamed: objself objSuperclassId
     ifAbsent: [nil].
       objsuperclass isNil
         ifFalse:
           [ objself
                 objIVs: (objself computeNewIVFrom: objsuperclass objIVs
     with: objself objIVs)]
         ifTrue:
           [ objself objIVs: (objself computeNewIVFrom: #(#class) with:
     objself objIVs)].
       objself
           objKeywords: (objself generateKeywords: (objself objIVs
     copyWithout: #class)).
       objself objMethodDict: (IdentityDictionary new: 3).
       Obj declareClass: objself.
       objself'
```

Note that this method works without inheritance since the class `ObjObject` does not exist yet.

The primitive `defineAllocateMethodIn: anObjClass` defines in anObjClass passed as argument the objMethod `allocate`. This `allocate` method takes only one argument: the class for which a new instance is created as shown below:

```
defineAllocateMethodIn: class

    class
       addUnaryMethod: #allocate
       withBody: 'objself allocateAnInstance'
```

Its definition is simple, it just calls the primitive `allocateAnInstance`.

Following the same principle, define the primitive `defineNewMethodIn: anObjClass` that defines in anObjClass passed as argument the objMethod `new`. `new` takes two arguments: a class and an initargs-list. It invokes the objMethod `allocate` and `initialize`.

Your job.

Make sure that you read and execute the test method: `testManuallyCreateObjClassAllocate`

Remarks

Read carefully the following remarks below and the code.

- In the objMethod `manualObjClassStructure`, the instance variable inheritance is simulated. Indeed the instance variable array (that represents the instance variable of the class) contains `#class` that should normally be inherited from `ObjObject` as we will see in the third phase of the bootstrap.

- Note that the class is declared into the class repository using the method `declareClass:`.

- Note the method `#initialize` is method of the metaclass `ObjClass`: when you create a class the initialize method is invoked on a class! The `initialize` objMethod defined on `ObjClass` has two aspects: the first one deals with the initialization of the class like any other instance (first line). This behavior is normally done using a super call to invoke the `initialize` method defined in `ObjObject`. The final version of the `initialize` method will do it using perform. The second one deals with the initialization of classes: it performs the instance variable inheritance, then computes the keywords of the newly created class. Note in this final step that the keyword array does not contain the `#class:` keyword because we do not want to let the user modify the class of an object.

6.3   Creation of ObjObject

Now you are in the situation where you can create the first real and normal class of the system: the class `ObjObject`. To do that you send the message new to class `ObjClass` specifying that the class you are creating is named `#ObjObject` and only has one instance variable called `class`. Then you will add the methods defining the behavior shared by all the objects.

Your job: objObjectStructure

Implement/read the following primitive `objObjectStructure` that creates the
`ObjObject` by invoking the `new` message to the class `ObjClass`:

```
Obj class >> objObjectStructure

   ^ (self giveClassNamed: #ObjClass)
      send: #new
      withArguments: #(#(#name: #ObjObject #iv: #(#class)))
```

The class `ObjObject` is named `ObjObject`, has only one instance variable `class`,
and does not have a superclass because it is the root of the inheritance graph.

Your job: createObjObject

Now implement the primitive `createObjObject` that calls `objObjectStruc-`
`ture` to obtain the `objObject` representing`objObject` class and define methods in it. To help you we give here the beginning of such a method

```
Obj class >> createObjObject
   | objObject |
   objObject := self objObjectStructure.
   objObject addUnaryMethod: #class withBody: 'objself objClass'.
   objObject addUnaryMethod: #isClass withBody: 'false'.
   objObject addUnaryMethod: #isMetaclass withBody: 'false'.
   ...
   ...
   ^ objObject
```

Implement the following methods in `ObjObject`

- the objMethod `class` that given an objInstance returns its class (the objInstance that represents the class).

- the objMethod `isClass` that returns false.

- the objMethod `isMetaClass` that returns false.

- the objMethod `error` that takes two arguments the receiver and the selector of the original invocation and raises an error.

- the objMethod `getIV` that takes the receiver and an attribute name,
  aSymbol, and returns its value for the receiver.

- the objMethod `setIV` that takes the receiver, an attribute name and a
  value and sets the value of the given attribute to the given value.

- the objMethod `initialize` that takes the receiver and an initargs-list
  and initializes the receiver according to the specification given by the

initargs-list. Note that here the `initialize` method only fills the instance according to the specification given by the initargs-list. Compare with the `initialize` method defined on `ObjClass`.

Make sure that you read and execute the test method: `testCreateObjObject-Structure`

In particular, notice that this class does not implement the class method `new` because it is not a metaclass but does implement the instance method `initialize` because any object should be initialized.

Your job: run the tests

- Make sure that you read and execute the test method: `testCreateOb-jObjectMessage`

- Make sure that you read and execute the test method: `testCreateOb-jObjectInstanceMessage`

6.4 Creation of ObjClass

Following the same approach, you can now recreate completely the class `ObjClass`. The primitive `createObjClass` is responsible for creating the final class `ObjClass`. So you will implement it and define all the primitives it needs. Now we only define what is specific to classes, the rest is inherited from the superclass of the class `ObjClass`, the class `ObjObject`.

```
Obj class >> createObjClass
   "self bootstrap"

   | objClass |
   objClass := self objClassStructure.
   self defineAllocateMethodIn: objClass.
   self defineNewMethodIn: objClass.
   self defineInitializeMethodIn: objClass.
   objClass
     addUnaryMethod: #isMetaclass
     withBody: 'objself objIVs includes: #superclass'.
  "an object is a class if is class is a metaclass. cool"

   objClass
     addUnaryMethod: #isClass
     withBody: 'objself objClass send: #isMetaclass withArguments:#()'.

   ^ objClass
```

To make the method `createObjClass` work we should implement the method it calls. Implement then:

- the primitive `objClassStructure` that creates the `ObjClass` class by invoking the new message to the class `ObjClass`. Note that during this method the `ObjClass` symbol refers to two different entities because the new class that is created using the old one is declared in the class dictionary with the same name.

Your job.

Make sure that you read and execute the test method: `testCreateObjClassStructure`. Now implement the primitive `createObjClass` that starts as follow:

```
Obj class >> createObjClass

    | objClass |
    objClass := self objClassStructure.
    self defineAllocateMethodIn: objClass.
    self defineNewMethodIn: objClass.
    self defineInitializeMethodIn: objClass.
    ...
    ^ objClass
```

Also define the following methods:

- the objMethod `isClass` that returns true.

- the objMethod `isMetaclass` that returns true.

```
objClass
    addUnaryMethod: #isMetaclass
    withBody: 'objself objIVs includes: #superclass'.

    "an object is a class if is class is a metaclass. cool"
```

```
objClass
    addUnaryMethod: #isClass
    withBody: 'objself objClass send: #isMetaclass withArguments:#()'.
```

- the primitive `defineInitializeMethodIn: anObjClass` that adds the objMethod `initialize` to the objClass passed as argument. The objMethod `initialize` takes the receiver (an objClass) and an initargs-list and initializesthe receiver according to the specification given by the initargs-list. In particular, it should be initialized as any other object, then it should compute its instance variable (i.e., inherited instance variables are computed), the keywords are also computed, the method dictionary should be defined and the class is then declared as an existing one. We provide the following template to help you.

```
Obj class>>defineInitializeMethodIn: objClass

   objClass
     addMethod: #initialize
     args: 'initArray'
     withBody:
        'objself super: #initialize withArguments: {initArray} from:
     superclassOfClassDefiningTheMethod.
         objself objIVs: (objself
                 computeNewIVFrom:
                       (Obj giveClassNamed: objself objSuperclassId)
       objIVs
                 with: objself objIVs).
         objself computeAndSetKeywords.
         objself objMethodDict: IdentityDictionary new.
         Obj declareClass: objself.
         objself'
```

```
Obj class >> defineInitializeMethodIn: objClass

   objClass
     addMethod: #initialize
     args: 'initArray'
     withBody:
        'objself super: #initialize withArguments: {initArray} from:
     superclassOfClassDefiningTheMethod.
         objself objIVs: (objself
            computeNewIVFrom: (Obj giveClassNamed: objself
     objSuperclassId) objIVs
            with: objself objIVs).
         objself computeAndSetKeywords.
         objself objMethodDict: IdentityDictionary new.
         Obj declareClass: objself.
         objself'
```

Your job.

Make sure that you execute the test method: `testCreateObjClassMessage.`

Note the following points:

- The locally specified instance variables now are just the instance variables that describe a class. The instance variable `class` is inherited from `ObjObject`.

- The `initialize` method now does a super send to invoke the initialization performed by `ObjObject`.

6.5 **First User Classes: ObjPoint**

Now that ObjVLisp is created and we can start to program some classes. Implement the class `ObjPoint` and `ObjColoredPoint`. Here is a possible implementation.

You can choose to implement it at the class level of the class Obj or even better in class named `ObjPointTest`.

Pay attention that your scenario covers the following aspects:

- First just create the class `ObjPoint`.

- Create an instance of the class `ObjPoint`.

- Send some messages defined in `ObjObject` to this instance.

Define the class `ObjPoint` so that we can create points as below (create a Pharo method to define it).

```
ObjClass send: #new
   withArguments: #((#name: #ObjPoint #iv: #(#x y) #superclass:
   #ObjObject)).
```

```
aPoint := pointClass send: #new withArguments: #((#x: 24 #y: 6)).
aPoint send: #getIV withArguments: #(#x).
aPoint send: #setIV withArguments: #(#x 25).
aPoint send: #getIV withArguments: #(#x).
```

Then add some functionality to the class `ObjPoint` like the methods x, x:, `display` which prints the receiver.

```
Obj ObjPoint
   addUnaryMethod: #givex
   withBody: 'objself valueOfInstanceVariable: #x '.
Obj ObjPoint
   addUnaryMethod: #display
   withBody:
    'Transcript cr;
      show: ''aPoint with x - ''.
    Transcript show: (objself send: #givex withArguments: #())
    printString;
   cr'.
```

Then test these new functionalities.

```
aPoint send: #x withArguments: #().
aPoint send: #x: withArguments: #(33).
aPoint send: #display withArguments: #().
```

6.6 First User Classes: ObjColoredPoint

Following the same idea, define the class `ObjColored`.

Create an instance and send it some basic messages.

```
aColoredPoint := coloredPointClass
    send: #new
    withArguments: #((#x: 24 #y: 6 #color: #blue)).
```

```
aColoredPoint send: #getIV withArguments: #(#x).
aColoredPoint send: #setIV withArguments: #(#x 25).
aColoredPoint send: #getIV withArguments: #(#x).
aColoredPoint send: #getIV withArguments: #(#color).
```

Your job.

Define some functionality and invoke them: the method color, implement the
method display so that it invokes the superclass and adds some information
related to the color. Here is an example:

```
coloredPointClass addUnaryMethod: #display
    withBody:
      'objself super: #display withArguments: #() from:
    superclassOfClassDefiningTheMethod.
      Transcript cr;
        show: '' with Color = ''.
      Transcript show: (objself send: #giveColor withArguments: #())
    printString; cr'.
```

```
aColoredPoint send: #x withArguments: #().
aColoredPoint send: #color withArguments: #().
aColoredPoint send: #display withArguments: #()
```

6.7 A First User Metaclass: ObjAbstract

Now implement the metaclass `ObjAbstract` that defines instances (classes)
that are abstract i.e., that cannot create instances. This class should raise an
error when it executes the new message.

Then the following shows you a possible use of this metaclass.

```
ObjAbstractClass
    send: #new
    withArguments: #(#(#name: #ObjAbstractPoint
            #iv: #()
            #superclass: #ObjPoint)).
```

```
ObjAbstractPoint send: #new
   withArguments: #(#(#x: 24 #y: 6))          "should raise an error"
```

You should redefine the new method. Note that the `ObjAbstractClass` is an instance of `ObjClass` because this is a class and inherits from it because this is a metaclass.

6.8   New features that you could implement

You can implement some simple features:

- define a metaclass that automatically defines accessors for the specified instances variables.

- avoid that we can change the selector and the arguments when calling a super send.

Shared Variables

Note that contrary to the proposition made in the 6th postulate of the original ObjVLisp model, class instance variables are not equivalent to shared variables. According to the 6th postulate, a shared variable will be stored in the instance representing the class and not in an instance variable of the class representing the shared variables. For example, if a workstation has a shared variable named `domain`. But the domain should not be an extra instance variable of the class of `Workstation`. Indeed domain has nothing to do with class description.

The correct solution is that `domain` is a value held into the list of the shared variable of the class `Workstation`. This means that a *class* has extra information to describe it: an instance variable `sharedVariable` holding pairs. So we should be able to write:

```
Obj Workstation getIV: #sharedVariable
or
Obj Workstation sharedVariableValue: #domain

and get
 #((domain 'inria.fr'))
```

Introduce shared variables: add a new instance variable in the class `ObjClass` to hold a dictionary of shared variable bindings (a symbol and a value) that can be queried using specific methods:`sharedVariableValue:` and `sharedVariableValue:put:`.

CHAPTER 7

Selected definitions

Smith was the first to introduce reflection in a programming language with
3Lisp. He defines reflection as:

- An entity's integral ability to represent, operate on, and otherwise deal
  with itself in the same way that it represents, operates on, and deals with
  its primary subject matter.

In the context of meta-object protocols, Bobrow refines the definition as follows:

- Reflection is the ability of a program to manipulate as data, something
  representing the state of the program during its own execution. There
  are two aspects of such manipulation: *introspection* and *intercession* (...)
  Both aspects require a mechanism for encoding the execution state as
  data; providing such an encoding is called *reification*.

Maes proposed some definitions for reflexive programming:

- A *computational system* is something that *reasons* about and *acts* upon
  some part of the world, called the *domain* of the system.

- A computational system may also be *causally connected* to its domain. This
  means that the system and its domain are linked in such a way that if one
  of the two changes, this leads to an effect upon the other.

- A *meta-system* is a computational system that has as its domain another
  computational system, called its *object-system*. (...) A meta-system has
  a representation of its object-system in its data. Its program specifies
  meta-computation about the object-system and is therefore called a *meta-
  program*.

- *Reflection* is the process of reasoning about and/or acting upon oneself.

- A *reflective system* is a causally connected meta-system that has as object-system itself. The data of a reflective system contain, besides the representation of some part of the external world, also a causally connected representation of itself, called *self-representation* of the system. [...] When a system is reasoning or acting upon itself, we speak of *reflective computation.*

- A language with a *reflective architecture* is a language in which all systems have access to a causally connected representation of themselves.

- A programming environment has a *meta-level architecture* if it has an architecture that supports meta-computation, without supporting reflective computation.

- The *meta-object* of an object X represents the explicit information about X (e.g. about its behavior and its implementation). The object X itself groups the information about the entity of the domain it represents.

Bibliography

[1] A. P. Black, S. Ducasse, O. Nierstrasz, D. Pollet, D. Cassou, and M. Denker. *Pharo by Example*. Square Bracket Associates, Kehrsatz, Switzerland, 2009.

[2] N. Bouraqadi, T. Ledoux, and F. Rivard. Safe metaclass programming. In *Proceedings OOPSLA '98*, pages 84–96, 1998.

[3] P. Cointe. Metaclasses are first class: the ObjVlisp model. In *Proceedings OOPSLA '87, ACM SIGPLAN Notices*, volume 22, pages 156–167, Dec. 1987.

[4] I. R. Forman and S. Danforth. *Putting Metaclasses to Work: A New Dimension in Object-Oriented Programming*. Addison-Wesley, 1999.

[5] G. Kiczales, J. des Rivières, and D. G. Bobrow. *The Art of the Metaobject Protocol*. MIT Press, 1991.

[6] B. Meyer. *Object-oriented Software Construction*. Prentice-Hall, 1988.

[7] G. L. Steele. *Common Lisp The Language*. Digital Press, second edition, 1990.